HEALING OUR HURTS
COPING WITH DIFFICULT EMOTIONS

Smyth & Helwys Publishing, Inc.
6316 Peake Road
Macon, Georgia 31210-3960
1-800-747-3016
©2012 by Daniel Bagby
All rights reserved.
Printed in the United States of America.

The paper used in this publication meets the minimum requirements of
American National Standard for Information Sciences—
Permanence of Paper for Printed Library Materials.
ANSI Z39.48–1984. (alk. paper)

Library of Congress Cataloging-in-Publication Data

Bagby, Daniel G.
Healing our hurts : coping with difficult emotions / by Daniel Bagby.
pages cm
ISBN 978-1-57312-613-7 (alk. paper)
1. Emotions--Religious aspects--Christianity. 2. Christian life. I. Title.
BV4597.3.B33 2012
248.4--dc23

2011048497

Disclaimer of Liability: With respect to statements of opinion or fact available in this work of nonfiction, Smyth & Helwys Publishing Inc. nor any of its employees, makes any warranty, express or implied, or assumes any legal liability or responsibility for the accuracy or completeness of any information disclosed, or represents that its use would not infringe privately-owned rights.

Sandy Morrison

HEALING OUR HURTS

COPING WITH DIFFICULT EMOTIONS

DANIEL **BAGBY**

Also by Daniel Bagby

Understanding Anger in the Church
Transition and Newness
Before You Marry
The Church: The Power to Help and to Hurt
Seeing Through Our Tears
Crisis Ministry: A Handbook
Beyond the Myths: The Journey to Adulthood

The Church and Addiction (editor)
Pastoral Responses to Sexual Abuse (editor)
Pastoral Responses to Suicide (editor)

Dedication

To Janet
Whose patience and grace has allowed me to write for years

Contents

Preface	xi
Introduction	1
Difficult Emotions	1
Assumptions	1
Chapter 1: Anger	5
What Usually Generates Anger?	6
Anger: Biblical Encounters	9
Practical Suggestions for Responding to Anger	10
Dealing with Other People's Anger	11
Dealing with Our Own Anger	15
Questions for Personal Reflection	16
Chapter 2: Anxiety	17
What Usually Generates Anxiety?	17
Anxiety: Biblical Encounters	19
Practical Suggestions for Responding to Anxiety	20
Dealing with Other People's Anxiety	22
Dealing with Our Own Anxiety	23
Questions for Personal Reflection	24
Chapter 3: Apathy	25
What Usually Generates Apathy?	25
Apathy: Biblical Encounters	26
Practical Suggestions for Responding to Apathy	28
Dealing with Other People's Apathy	29
Dealing with Our Own Apathy	31
Questions for Personal Reflection	33
Chapter 4: Despair	35
What Usually Generates Despair?	36
Despair: Biblical Encounters	36
Practical Suggestions for Responding to Despair	38

Dealing with Other People's Despair	40
Dealing with Our Own Despair	41
Questions for Personal Reflection	43

Chapter 5: Doubt — 45
What Usually Generates Doubt?	46
Doubt: Biblical Encounters	46
Practical Suggestions for Responding to Doubt	48
Dealing with Other People's Doubt	50
Dealing with Our Own Doubt	51
Questions for Personal Reflection	52

Chapter 6: Envy — 53
What Usually Generates Envy?	53
Envy: Biblical Encounters	54
Practical Suggestions for Responding to Envy	55
Dealing with Other People's Envy	56
Dealing with Our Own Envy	57
Questions for Personal Reflection	58

Chapter 7: Fear — 59
What Usually Generates Fear?	59
Fear: Biblical Encounters	60
Practical Suggestions for Responding to Fear	61
Dealing with Other People's Fear	63
Dealing with Our Own Fear	64
Questions for Personal Reflection	66

Chapter 8: Frustration — 67
What Usually Generates Frustration?	67
Frustration: Biblical Encounters	68
Practical Suggestions for Responding to Frustration	69
Dealing with Other People's Frustration	70
Dealing with Our Own Frustration	71
Questions for Personal Reflection	72

Chapter 9: Guilt 73
    What Usually Generates Guilt? 73
    Guilt: Biblical Encounters 74
    Practical Suggestions for Responding to Guilt 75
    Dealing with Other People's Guilt 77
    Dealing with Our Own Guilt 78
    Questions for Personal Reflection 79

Chapter 10: Passion 81
    What Usually Generates Passion? 81
    Passion: Biblical Encounters 81
    Practical Suggestions for Responding to Passion .. 83
    Dealing with Other People's Passion 86
    Dealing with Our Own Passion 87
    Questions for Personal Reflection 88

Chapter 11: Shame 89
    What Usually Generates Shame? 89
    Shame: Biblical Encounters 90
    Practical Suggestions for Responding to Shame ... 91
    Dealing with Other People's Shame 93
    Dealing with Our Own Shame 94
    Questions for Personal Reflection 95

Chapter 12: Sorrow 97
    What Usually Generates Sorrow? 97
    Sorrow: Biblical Encounters 99
    Practical Suggestions for Responding to Sorrow . 101
    Dealing with Other People's Sorrow 103
    Dealing with Our Own Sorrow 103
    Questions for Personal Reflection 105

Chapter 13: Stress 107
    What Usually Generates Stress? 108
    Stress: Three Biblical Encounters 108
    Practical Suggestions for Responding to Stress ... 109
    Dealing with Other People's Stress 111

Dealing with Our Own Stress	112
Questions for Personal Reflection	113

Chapter 14: Suspicion	**115**
What Usually Generates Suspicion?	115
Suspicion: Biblical Encounters	116
Practical Suggestions for Responding to Suspicion	118
Dealing with Other People's Suspicion	119
Dealing with Our Own Suspicion	120
Questions for Personal Reflection	121

Preface

These pages identify ways to care for and respond to some of the prevailing emotions that church folks and other caregivers face in their nurture of people. The list is not exhaustive. I hope that the suggested initiatives and responses may be of value to any reader who is committed to the care of the variety of human emotions that color the journey of God's people from birth to death. May God's wisdom and insight provide strength and understanding for each experience, and may the power and value of each emotion bring joy and perspective in life!

—Daniel G. Bagby
Ted Adams Emeritus Professor of Pastoral Care
Baptist Theological Seminary at Richmond

Introduction

Difficult Emotions

There are a number of challenging emotions in the journey of human relationships. People of all ages struggle with understanding the variety of complex feelings we share. We wonder what some of these emotions mean, how to handle them responsibly, and how to respond to them in relationships. A cluster of these complicated emotions are especially bewildering to believers, who struggle to live as redemptive disciples in a reactive world. For some believers, the most difficult emotions to manage are anger, anxiety, apathy, despair, doubt, envy, fear, frustration, guilt, passion, shame, sorrow, stress, and suspicion.

Because all of these emotions can be a source of distress and challenge, and because they are all evident in a variety of biblical encounters, I have attempted in the following pages to provide perspective to caregivers and others who must deal regularly with intense emotions in a redemptive and responsible way. Three specific goals shape the following pages: (1) to identify and explain some of the dynamics in several complex human emotions; (2) to offer practical biblical insights to these feelings; and (3) to interpret faith-based responses that offer useful perspectives for people responding to challenging human interactions.

Assumptions

Several assumptions shape our study of personal human interactions, and identifying them will help the reader understand the material and my point of departure. First of all, I assume that *all emotions discussed here are created by God and therefore have a redemptive purpose at their source.* A second assumption I hold is that *the Bible offers us useful insight into the proper stewardship of emotions, and that emotions may become either our allies or our enemies in the course of daily living, depending on how we express or manage them.*

A third assumption I make here is that *we were not born with certain automatic emotional responses to specific feelings or situations, but that we have learned these responses over a long period of time, mostly from our family—usually first by observation and then by imitation of them in practice.* The home in which we grew up is the first "school" where we were taught how adults express and respond to feelings.

Another assumption in these pages is that *you and I are only in control of how we express our own feelings to another person; we are not in control of how someone else expresses feelings.* Each of us is responsible both for the emotions we hold and for how we express them, but I believe that I neither create nor control other people's emotions.

On the other hand—and this is an additional assumption I make—*you and I are capable of controlling and changing our own emotional responses to situations.* We can learn to alter or change our emotional responses to particular experiences. We can learn to act more effectively in expressing specific feelings. We can also learn how to respond redemptively to the emotions of others.

We work best, therefore, when we focus on our own emotions and behaviors rather than try to change someone else's emotions. I believe that we can *suggest* ways in which someone else can alter responses or feelings, and we can recommend certain controls and boundaries for those who struggle with intense emotions. But each of us works most effectively in the care of emotions by taking responsibility for how we ourselves express or respond to a variety of feelings.

One additional assumption I hold may need to be emphasized: *Hard work and determination are essential elements in learning better ways to cope with strong feelings.* Many of us have learned inadequate or inappropriate ways to deal with intense emotions, and only hard work and a deep commitment to unlearn those ineffective responses will succeed in changing our behavior. I further believe that Christians are not required to struggle alone with these issues. All of us have access to the healing Presence of God, who helps us "in our weakness" and guides us into paths of peace and wholeness—for God's sake and for ours (2 Cor 12:9; Ps 23:3). The Spirit of God is an ally in our expression of all emotions, and the Bible can assist us in discovering those insights and responses God would have us know and learn.

Each of us has a personal history with strong emotions. We have struggled with powerful feelings precisely because they are intense and important. We have learned to fear strong emotions perhaps because we have been offered few effective ways to deal with them. Sometimes we have sidestepped challenging emotions because the communities in which we grew up gave us little positive help in coping effectively with such feelings. Most of us have considerable anxiety about dealing with "charged" issues anyway, and we may have felt helpless to control or contain some of our own responses.

One more challenge may need to be identified in the care of relationships. Some folks have stumbled across an unexpected benefit in the particular way they have dealt with strong feelings and may feel reluctant to give up their "discovered" advantage. (People who gain distance from others by seeming aloof and apathetic, for example, often discover a benefit in being left alone. Those who display explosive emotions create a "space" for themselves by "blowing up" when they feel threatened, and thus gain safety in the added distance.) The people who will benefit most from reading these pages, therefore, are the ones who seek a more effective way to manage strong emotions—and who want to learn how to respond more effectively to the feelings of others.

Let's begin by examining the emotions that appear to trouble us most. How can we manage them and channel them most responsibly? The following chapters will focus on each of several significant emotions at work in the Bible, explain their purpose and challenge, and suggest ways to handle each set of feelings in a responsible way.

Chapter 1

Anger

Anger is probably the most feared and misunderstood of all human emotions. Biblically, anger is neither described as a sin in itself nor identified as a "bad" emotion. In the Old Testament (Exod 4:14; Num 11:10; Deut 6:15; Ps 7:6; Isa 5:25, etc.) and in the New Testament (Mark 3:5; 9:19; John 2:15-16; Eph 4:26, etc.), both God and Jesus are reported as being angry several times. According to the Scriptures, anger itself is not good or bad. What we do with our anger results in either constructive or destructive behavior. Anger can be an expression of deep care over an issue or a just cause, or passion over a wrong committed or an injustice ignored.

Anger can function as a deep concern over the abuse or neglect of a defenseless individual. This bold emotion can be employed in the cause of good or ill. Strong feelings properly channeled can become instruments of care (as when God expressed anger at Israel not to reject that people but to bring them to responsible account; or when Jesus expressed anger with religious leaders in order to keep them from exploiting vulnerable people). On the other hand, inappropriately handled strong emotions become an enemy of grace and a cause for concern and control (Cain killing Abel, Moses losing his temper, Peter attacking a servant). The Bible eloquently describes the destructive results of unbridled anger, documenting its capacity to generate harm (Gen 37:18ff; Exod 2:12; 1 Sam 18:8; Jonah 4:1-3; Matt 26:51ff; Acts 7:54).

Our first "models" for expressing anger are often our parents. From parents or significant other adults, we learned our initial emotional responses to the events of life. Depending on how our first heroes or models expressed this intense emotion, we have learned either healthy or destructive ways to express anger ourselves.

As I wrote in 1978 in a book called *Understanding Anger in the Church*, many people have an unpleasant experience with anger and how it was "shared" at home. Our most unhappy experiences with anger tend to involve some form of abuse or loss of control by an adult, bruised or broken relationships, fear and intimidation, high degrees of stress, or hostile and invasive behaviors that left us frustrated or even injured.

People who display intense anger are obviously emotionally engaged. An issue of deep concern may have triggered their feelings. A perceived wrong or slight may have ignited their passion. Dated or unresolved expectations may occasion angry responses. These individuals may have learned to use anger as a way of creating "space" by intimidating a bystander—in response to feeling intimidated themselves.

Unfortunately, people who express anger openly can also overwhelm, distress, injure, or scare us. Our own challenge in dealing with anger often resides in the history of accumulated bad experiences most of us have with this chief of emotions. Our memory banks are full of painful and unhealthy encounters with anger, and we must first understand those stored memories in order to sort out the healthy and unhealthy ways we have learned to respond to anger.

What Usually Generates Anger?

What memories are still at work in our minds when we deal with anger? Many of us have had our share of unpleasant experiences with this emotion. Memories tend to cluster in groups of five or six important reactions when we face anger: anxiety, fear, frustration, intimidation, pain, or rejection. What baggage does each memory bring to the surface when we encounter anger?

Sometimes we respond with anger when we are *anxious*. If we strive for comfort and peace of mind, the reversal of that sense of calm can cause significant stress. Personal equilibrium is a valued human goal; anxiety dislodges our fragile emotional and spiritual balance and makes us feel vulnerable. The discomfort of losing control can make us recall unpleasant childhood moments when we felt unease, and the emotional history of those distressing memories can return to the surface with an intensity that troubles us and evokes an inflamed passion.

Fear is another personal dynamic that triggers displays of anger. When afraid, we may respond in anger as a protective, intense emotion because we feel out of control and don't know what to do next. If we have been scared by an out-of-control adult who vented strong emotions during our childhood, we may retain those fears for a lifetime. We may have feared for our own safety; we may have feared that the person would harm someone else—or even themselves; we may also have feared that we, too, might lose control over our emotions; or we may fear the reoccurrence of the emotional or physical abuse that accompanied angry outbursts we experienced in childhood. The difference between anxiety and fear is that anxiety is a generalized, unspecified dread of an unknown harm, while fear is the dread of a specific and identified harm.

Frustration often accompanies eruptions of anger because recurring, unsuccessful attempts to resolve an issue or complete a task evoke a sense of defeat or failure and distract us from focused, rational responses. Anger can take over and become the main event in a situation, displacing an original issue or goal in favor of focusing on the emotion itself. Frustration can be distracting when people use anger as a way of sidestepping primary issues or avoiding a subject altogether. Anger becomes a response to a frustration when we cannot address an issue—or have no control over its resolution—so that the angry response replaces the issue itself. Intense emotions often trump original issues, and we struggle with our helplessness to prevent it.

Sometimes distressed or highly stressed people may employ anger as a way of *intimidating* others. Frightened people need emotional space in order to manage their insecurities, and they often raise their voices and levels of intensity in an attempt to create a safe distance from others or control the actions of people around them. Some frightened people resort to anger as a "scatter bomb" technique, dumping out a barrage of emotions as a means of clearing the area. The other party is too intimidated to respond.

Anger has also emerged in response to our *pain*. We naturally seek to avoid physical or emotional pain. If anger in our emotional history was partnered with actions that caused physical pain, especially in abusive relationships, many of us learned quickly to seek protection and to act cautiously during such outbursts. Emotional pain, though less apparent, can act as a significant deterrent to dialogue in a relationship. What child will forget the strident voice that belittles and hurts? If as children we found it harder to protect ourselves from the injustice of violent anger, as teenagers and adults we begin to look for more effective ways to avoid being vulnerable. It is not only appropriate to seek asylum from physical or emotional pain; it is normal to respond to such abuse with reactions of deep anger and challenge.

Angry words and behaviors can also signal a feeling of *rejection*. People who are angry often send messages of rejection with their intense behavior. Angry people have felt rejection and tend to create experiences in which they reject others. The emotional message in such encounters is often, "I'm expecting you to reject me anyway, so I'll reject you before you reject me." Anger is thus a self-protective device when people feel insecure or uncertain. Children learn quickly to personalize angry words and behaviors as signals of personal rejection. Carried into adulthood, such signals deliver a dated message of rejection to the listener. Some angry manifestations are based on an unfortunate internal message: "I feel rejected or unvalued, so I will demean you to feel better about myself." Unfortunately, anger prevents us from exploring a relationship behind the bravado of the noise—or the "bite"—of another person.

Clearly, there are valid reasons that anger is a difficult emotion to understand. A frequently present emotion in the biblical record, anger has many different facets and expressions. Now we will consider a selective list of passages in the Bible that speak to this emotion.

Anger: Biblical Encounters

What caused Cain to turn on his brother, Abel, and kill him? Early in the pages of Genesis we discover this sad evidence of anger turned destructively on another human being. There is no way to interpret Cain's violent act without acknowledging that anger played an important role in his behavior. Was jealousy the primary issue at work, or did Cain react to the bitter sting of perceived rejection by God, who had accepted Abel's offering but dismissed Cain's? We don't know, but we can all identify with the pain of personal rejection.

What anger was at work when Moses threw onto the ground—and broke—the tablets with God's Commandments in response to his frustration over the Israelites' idolatry and fickleness (Exod 32:19)? His response to the faithlessness of his companions was at best destructive, even if spontaneous. God instructed the prophet to secure a second set of tablets (Exod 34) and reminded him that he had broken the first set. Was Moses so angry with his companions that he forgot the value of the stones in his hands, or did he break them to dramatize the brokenness of their covenant with God? We don't know, but the Scriptures clearly declare that his anger took control of him.

Was anger or revenge at work in Samson's request of God for strength to "bring down the house" upon his Philistine captors, killing not only "more than he slew in his life" (Judg 16:30) but causing his own death (self anger)? Was his behavior a model to be followed, or was his action a destructive example of how not to express one's anger?

What are some practical first steps that can assist us to better deal with and respond to some of these challenging displays of anger? Given how deeply angry emotions affect us, how can we deal with anger in a constructive way? Here are a few recommendations.

Practical Suggestions for Responding to Anger

"Do you know when anyone from that congregation calls me? They call me once a year. Yeah, you guessed it! They call me once a year to ask me for my money. That's the only time I hear from anyone there. I don't think they care whether I show up or not—as long as I send them my money." (Long pause.) "I'm through with it," he added.

I had come to Jim's house after I called him and asked for permission to do so. He was on a short list of church members who had not attended any church services for quite some time, and the deacon body had identified him as one of several people who were most likely not only detached but also alienated from the church. I had asked the deacons (1) to help me identify a group of absent members who might need attention and initiative in order for us to express care for them, (2) to learn from them if they still wanted a relationship with our congregation, and (3) to see if the church was the cause of their distancing or feelings of offense. One of my hopes was to learn how a congregation might respond better to church members who had once been active but lately had neglected contact and participation in church work.

This situation with Jim helped me remember the following lessons about responding to an angry person.

1. You don't need to respond to anger with anger. Angry responses rarely produce positive results or foster communication. Just because someone is angry in front of you doesn't mean you have to become angry yourself. You don't need to feel responsible for someone else's anger. People become angry for many reasons, so don't take responsibility for someone else's feelings. You are only responsible for your part in a conversation. Sometimes angry people don't listen well and are not interested in what you have to say. You can only invite people to a dialogue—you cannot force them into one. You are only responsible for offering people options or choices for how they might deal with their anger. You are not responsible for the choices they make or for the feelings or responses they express!

2. It is often more effective to respond calmly to angry comments and identify the useful aspects of the encounter: "Whatever you are disturbed about is very important to you, or you wouldn't feel as strongly as you do. Can you tell me what is most disturbing about this to you right now?" If the person persists in expressing passionate, angry feelings and seems out of control, try an adult version of "time out": "This is obviously very important to you, and you feel deeply about it, but I think I need to back away right now and wait for a time when I can talk to you about this without the heavy feelings of the moment. Let's get back to this after we let it settle so that it's not as heavy as it sounds to me right now."

3. Remember that anger is often the first passion expressed by a person who cares, fears, or is frustrated. We show strong feelings because we care, we are afraid, or we feel that we have no control over a situation. Responding to the underlying emotion is more helpful than taking anger at face value. Behind some angry comments are people's fears that they are not being taken seriously, or their deep passion or belief about an issue or cause they believe is at stake, or a sense that they may be losing control over some important dimension of their lives.

4. Remember that anger is sometimes a veiled request for someone to acknowledge a person's deep frustration about certain things he or she knows can't be changed. Angry people may just want someone else to validate their distress or pain over some injustice or occurrence over which they have no control. They want a "witness" to their loss and want someone to take them seriously by listening to them.

5. Pray for people who are burdened by their intense feelings. They may rail in anger because that was the only way they've been taken seriously in the past.

Dealing with Other People's Anger

The first question we must answer in the face of anger is whether we have the coping capacity to deal with this volatile emotion. We have an obligation to ourselves in dealing with any kind of emotion. If we have a limited capacity to cope effectively with certain feelings, we have no business trying to field those emotions in another person. If coping with someone's anger is a paralyzing or oppressive experience for us, we need to protect ourselves. We can't care for others until we learn how to care for ourselves.

If feelings of anger temporarily overwhelm or incapacitate us, we should immediately remove ourselves from the situation or environment in which they are occurring. Feelings that overpower us make it difficult for us to hear well, respond well, or function well. We are less capable of rational or reasoned responses when we are afraid, anxious, or intimidated. If we are overwhelmed by someone's anger, our best first step is to withdraw physically to give ourselves emotional space and create safety.

Gaining physical and emotional space affords us a better position from which to ask ourselves basic questions about our reactions to anger. We can take note of our physiological responses to anger: Is my heart beating faster, my pulse quickened? Is my breathing altered, or has my body gone into a sense of general alert—drier mouth, flushed cheeks, stiffening muscles? (These are all normal physiological signs of stress when we feel unsafe or off balance.) Any of these stress signals can be our ally in understanding a valid need to put physical distance between ourselves and someone else as a protective measure for personal survival—and recovery. A safe distance and some initial reflection on what is happening will assist us in limiting the toxic effects of an angry expression.

The next useful step in dealing with anger is to attempt to identify any repeating messages we have stored in our memories: (1) What do I think I heard? (2) Whom do I think is responsible for these feelings? (3) What do I believe I must do in response to what I have heard? These questions are essential for helping us ensure that we understood what was actually said. It is not uncommon to misunderstand the emotion behind a person's words. When we are stressed or anxious, we don't hear well, and strain and fear can distort our interpretation.

To answer the first question, then, means to try to discern the right message. Our best chance of getting it right may be to have the person repeat herself so that we may assess what she actually said. What often happens at this point in a conversation, however, is that, in the absence of any clearly stated meaning, we tend to interpret and respond without accurate information, and we insert our own inaccurate perceptions. For example, "She is angry with me because we're out of copying paper, and she thinks I should have ordered it" is an interpretation of someone saying, "What? We're out of copying paper and the report is due this morning!?" But that may not be an accurate interpretation of her anger. (She could be angry at herself for not checking the paper stock two days ago or for waiting until the last minute to prepare the report; or she could be angry at someone else who told her that they had ordered the paper, etc.)

There are several possible reasons for anger. What we need to guard against is the temptation to supply an incorrect interpretation to an angry outburst, and then to react emotionally to our *interpreted* version as if it were accurate. Psychologists sometimes call such invented interpretations "magical thinking." During early childhood, we make artificial connections between an event and our responsibility for it: "Mother is crying; I wonder what I did wrong now!" We "magically" assume that we are to blame for an occurrence simply because we were present when it took place. The capacity to distinguish between the occurrence of an event and our responsibility for it is a function of a thinking process that develops in our brains as we grow up. Such a distinction, or separation, is a learned experience—not automatic. Many adults never overcome the childhood habit of connecting two unrelated experiences as if one caused the other simply because they happened at the same time.

A second important question is whether we believe that we are responsible for someone else's feelings. This myth, again, is another misunderstanding learned during childhood. Somewhere along the way, many of us have been taught—and learned to believe—that we are the cause of someone else's feelings. Apart from physical injury we can inflict on someone else, we are not responsible for the feelings someone else has! Each person is responsible for his or her own feelings. How each of us responds to someone else's behavior is our own responsibility. We may respond in anger to a certain event or action, but that response is our chosen reaction. We have learned to respond in certain ways to certain events, and we alone are responsible for creating those feelings. I can respond to a personal verbal attack with indifference, amusement, or anger. Whichever way I choose to respond is a result of what I perceive and what feelings I choose to express. (Think of how often someone says, "You made me angry!" This is rarely the truth.)

Unfortunately, all of us have spent a lot of time and energy practicing certain learned responses to particular experiences, and we usually believe that those responses and feelings are "automatic" or "instinctive." The truth is that most of our responses and feelings are learned reactions. That is why we cannot be responsible for someone else's feelings. Each of us can only take responsibility for the way we react to a given occurrence. Understanding this truth will make it easier for us to appreciate that we are not to blame for someone else's anger, joy, indifference—or any other emotion they have.

Such an insight can protect us from the illusion that anyone's anger is our doing. How someone else reacts to something is his own responsibility and his own creation. We don't need to fear, therefore, that we are the creator of someone else's rage or frustration. They alone are responsible for their feelings.

It follows, then, to answer question 3, that if we are not to blame for someone else's feelings, then we are also not responsible for changing other people's feelings. We cannot, in fact, change anyone else's feelings at all! They are in charge of their own feelings and must choose how to respond. To answer this last "time-out" question, then, we don't need to fix or change or resolve other people's feelings because we are not responsible for their feelings—they are!

With each of these truths in mind, then, we can learn to respond to someone's anger in whatever way we wish! First of all, if a person is angry, she is responsible for her anger. Secondly, just because he is angry doesn't mean we must become angry, afraid, frustrated, or respond in any other way. And finally, we don't have to "fix" or change someone else's anger because we are not the cause of it, and we have no power to change it ourselves anyway.

Dealing with Our Own Anger

We not only have to respond to anger in other people; we must also deal with our own bouts of anger. A key question in managing our own anger is whether we have learned appropriate and responsible boundaries to its expression. How can we evaluate how responsibly and appropriately we manage our own experiences of anger?

What draws out your anger? It will help you to know what specific issues or events elicit an angry response from you. Each of us has learned to react in anger to certain things, and knowing what those things are for you can help you anticipate and manage an angry response. Some people, for example, have been taught—and believe—that being called particular words by someone else is a signal to respond angrily. When I worked as chaplain at a women's prison several years ago, it was not uncommon for an inmate to respond angrily to words someone else called her—and in the process get manipulated into a response (fight) that would cost her extended jail time. Only a few of those women learned that they were actually being "controlled" by someone else who could evoke a destructive reaction by simply saying a word or two. Knowing what causes our anger is a helpful insight into the issues to which we have been trained to react. What we tell ourselves we don't like may be a helpful clue about what we choose to be angry about.

What does my anger do to me physiologically and emotionally? The same symptoms of physiological stress mentioned earlier begin to show up when we are angry—including a state of agitation, increased blood pressure, adrenalin accelerating blood flow, flushed cheeks, etc.

QUESTIONS FOR PERSONAL REFLECTION

1. What about this issue is causing my anger?

2. When in the past has a similar event triggered this kind of response from me?

3. What have I done before that works best when I feel this way?

4. In what way do I benefit from this particular emotion?

Anxiety

One of our most common responses to change or discomfort is anxiety. It is the clearest message that we feel off balance, outside our emotional comfort zone, or even in danger. Anxiety is a general response of discomfort or dread, usually to a vague, unspecified threat. While fear usually describes our response to a specific, identified concern, anxiety is usually an emotional reaction to an unclear or unidentified apprehension. Like heat to a motor, anxiety produces a heightened awareness that increases our focus and caution, an internal set of alarms warning us of some potential harm or vulnerability. An excessive amount of anxiety becomes disturbing and destructive to our system or self.

We can identify physiological changes in our bodies when we become anxious. The first set of signals tends to include altered or shortened breathing, accelerated heart activity, muscular tensions, trembling, increased perspiration, increased circulatory activity, and sometimes a momentary incapacity to function. Emotionally, there is a perception of danger, a sense of helplessness, and a general feeling of discomfort.

What Usually Generates Anxiety?

Several experiences can trigger anxiety. Facing an unknown or unclear issue often generates physiological responses in us that we call anxiety. What some cultures have described as "angst" is often our response to the unexpected and unpredictable in life. Movie directors and play writers count on stimulating such responses in their audiences by placing heroes in mysterious or dangerous circumstances. In the entertainment world, the use of music and sound effects have the added function of elevating our "alarm" system in anticipation of an unknown, unpleasant happening.

Anxiety may also erupt when we perceive that we are facing an imminent danger. If we sense that we are vulnerable physically, emotionally, or at risk of harm in some other way, our discomfort level rises considerably. None of us wants to be in danger or susceptible to injury; if we perceive that we are being attacked, pressed, or assaulted, we react physiologically and emotionally—not to mention spiritually—to potential damage.

Change of any kind may give rise to an anxious response. We are accustomed to what is familiar, and we find comfort in sameness and predictability. When change occurs, we respond with anxiety as a way to recover a lost sense of balance. And since change is constant, each of us is always adjusting to new conditions and different circumstances by generating some physiological and emotional responses—and at times becoming anxious.

Loss of control also generates anxiety. Self-control is a matter of personal safety and security, and if we perceive that we are "out of control" in a given situation, we become more anxious. The same response occurs when we sense that we have lost control over a particular situation or in a relationship. Since we usually live with the myth that we are in control, any perception that we have lost control—or have no control—over a situation creates a certain amount of anxiety.

The threat of a primary loss or separation can also trigger significant anxiety. If we perceive that we are losing something or someone dear to us, we often respond with emotions that activate physiological promptings such as the ones mentioned above. Students of human behavior tell us that even from birth we experience significant discomfort when we experience major separation from sources of safety and security; this is described as "separation anxiety." Its psychological effect carries over developmentally from childhood into adulthood, so that various forms of separation from stability or security create anxious responses.

Comparing ourselves negatively to others may also generate anxiety. If I believe that I am the least productive person at work, the most ineffective student, the least attractive person in a group, or the most unlikely to succeed, I can render myself anxious. What therapists call "self-talk" can cause us internal agony since the negative messages we store and repeat to ourselves become the source of major distress. Our discomfort then is with ourselves, as we judge ourselves inferior and less valuable than others. Such judgments are heightened by the perception that we are helpless to change any aspects of our lives that we find distasteful or unacceptable. This emotion is not new. Let's explore a few examples of anxiety in the Bible.

Anxiety: Biblical Encounters

Sarai became anxious about her childless condition when God's promise of a child was delayed. In her discomfort, she proposed to Abram that he father a child by their maid Hagar. Her anxiety was only heightened when Hagar became pregnant with Ishmael, and a perplexed Abram allowed her to deal harshly with her servant (Gen 16:1-6).

An anxious Jacob, returning to face his betrayed brother, Esau, positioned many gifts and cattle ahead of him at his arrival, hoping to reduce Esau's potential bitterness for having his birthright stolen by Jacob. Restless as he crossed the Jabbok River, Jacob spent the night wrestling with himself and God (Gen 32:11-25).

Another restless spirit, Moses, encountering God through a sacred bush in a lonely place, was so anxious about returning to Egypt and representing a God he did not know well that he tried to argue with God about being chosen to lead the Israelites out of Egyptian captivity (Exod 3–4). Soon that newly freed and anxious people, less than halfway through the journey, feared for lack of food and complained to Moses that they had been better off in their captivity (Exod 16:2-3).

When Moses sent twelve spies to examine the promised land of Canaan, ten of the returning men were so consumed by anxiety that their report was one of fear and discouragement. Before Caleb and Joshua's "minority report" was followed, those ten messengers infected the congregation of Israelites enough that they elected captains in their midst to lead them back to Egypt (Num 13:27–14:8). Anxiety, like a fever, can be passed on by a few people to a large population that can quickly lose perspective and respond without the benefit of adequate information.

Joseph had to be reassured by a messenger from God that Mary's pregnancy should not be a cause for panic (Matt 1:20). Out of anxiety, Herod decided to have all the male children under age two killed in the vicinity of Jesus Christ's birthplace. His perceived threat of a competing Jewish "king" led to a mass assassination of innocent babies. Anxious scribes (Mark 2:6) and Pharisees responded to Jesus with suspicion and dread, unsure of what to do in the face of his popularity (John 12:19). Even his disciples displayed bouts with anxiety (Matt 14:28-30) and struggled to control their discomfort in the face of uncertainty (John 14:1-5).

Practical Suggestions for Responding to Anxiety

Her voice sounded tense over the telephone, and there was noticeable agitation in her delivery: "Pastor, we need to meet as soon as we can, or we're going to have a big problem on our hands! We need to sit down and talk as soon as you can! Can I come over right now? I've already talked with the associate pastor about this, and we need to deal with this soon or this thing is going to blow!"

"I'll be glad to sit down and talk with you and the associate pastor as soon as I can," I replied. "I've got some time in about an hour—and I can tell you are quite anxious about something. Is it okay if you tell me over the phone what the issue is about so I can see if I need to do any homework before you get here? Maybe I can look for an answer we need."

I was trying to reduce her anxiety as we talked, hoping I could calm her down even with the tone of my voice so she could drive safely halfway across town to meet us. "I also need to see if the associate pastor can meet us on that schedule, by the way, since I don't know her schedule," I added.

The woman came in, visibly agitated, her face flushed and lips tightened, and began pouring out her tale of distress over the behavior of a couple of church members who had corralled her and confronted her over a set of decisions in a recent committee meeting. She had reason to be anxious—she apparently had been verbally abused in the process. To help her and others like her, I use these steps.

1. One of the most effective antidotes to anxiety is slowing down enough to trace the source of the discomfort. Ask yourself, "What has created this unease?" If we find the source of the distress, we can begin to assess if it is accurate, valid, or relevant. Some anxious moments are created by inaccurate messages, and correcting the inaccuracy can reduce the resulting anxiety. If a doctor tells me that I have cancer, my anxiety level rises quickly. But if a second phone call from the lab reports that they had switched the test reports and that actually my test was clear, my anxiety is reduced.

If I interpret that everyone at work is performing better than I am, anxiety ensues. Feedback from a supervisor may give me a more accurate report, and my anxiety will be tempered by the discovery that I am actually performing better than I thought. Our own expectations and interpretations have a lot to do with the amount of anxiety we create for ourselves.

2. A second check on anxiety is to identify any issues over which we have no control. Sometimes we spend a lot of energy fretting over events or circumstances that we cannot control. Does any good come of mulling over issues we can do nothing about? The only brief value in reviewing such issues is if doing so is part of our process of letting go of them. Unfortunately, most of us have taught ourselves to return repeatedly to an unchanging issue we don't like, ruminating over our inability to affect it.

3. A third source of anxiety is a temptation to take too much responsibility for particular things. We often teach ourselves what some therapists call "overfunctioning," a term that refers to some people's tendency to become overly involved in the outcome of events, taking too much responsibility for things over which they had limited control. Ask yourself, "Have I taken more responsibility

(blame) for this than is expected? Why am I so emotionally involved in the outcome of this issue?"

4. Anxiety can also be curbed by paying attention to a personal list of experiences or circumstances that have increased our discomfort in the past. By noting our history of situations or events that have made us anxious over the years, we can take care to avoid some of those distressing experiences. Taking note of distressing experiences when we felt attacked, criticized, or demeaned growing up may alert us to current situations that evoke those painful emotions.

5. Some experiences that cause no anxiety in some people may be so unnerving to us that regularly avoiding them will reduce our feelings of distress. People whose anxiety peaks when they take speedy rides at theme parks, visit certain relatives, or speak in public can take precautions to control their exposure to such events. If specific occurrences create sizeable anxiety, we may need to limit how often we are exposed to them.

Dealing with Other People's Anxiety

Remember that most people respond to change with varying degrees of anxiety. Expect them to show signs of anxiety, especially if the changes are surprising, sudden, or unpleasant. Give people time to "collect themselves" when they are fielding different changes; do not rush them to respond to you, make decisions, or focus clearly on the moment. Take the time to inquire about someone's ability to cope and assess how many issues or events they are facing, then determine whether they are at their "absorption" capacity as you work with them.

Remember that perceived criticism or confrontation can generate enough discomfort to evoke a high degree of anxiety in a person, and that even moderate levels of anxiety reduce an individual's capacity to hear accurately or maintain perspective. Allow people who are anxious a few self-protective steps in their attempt to regain balance. Some folks become defensive when they feel anxious, but they will usually calm down if they don't feel pushed or attacked. Some people withdraw emotionally when perceiving themselves as off balance. Others, momentarily stunned, look for both space and time to regain self-control.

Such interruptions afford us a better chance to assess whether an anxious person can next hear and respond with a better perspective—or needs further rest and care—in order to function more effectively. Give such people permission to delay important decisions, if possible, and postpone any significant reengagement of anxiety-provoking issues.

Dealing with Our Own Anxiety

If you can identify the particular circumstances or issues that activate your physiological alerts, you will gain some advantage by anticipating experiences that provoke anxiety for you and then avoiding them as much as possible. Once you know what specific issues tend to trigger your anxiety, you may also begin to ask yourself what about those events creates your discomfort. Traumatizing events tend to lodge in our memories for years, acting as "emotional hotwires" that reawaken distressing emotions in the here and now.

As you can, try to separate what you are thinking at the moment from what is happening in front of you or is being said in front of you. Most of us have trained ourselves to believe that we are responsible for the actions or thoughts of other people. As mentioned in the chapter on anger, such "magical thinking" means that we tend to blame ourselves for how other people act or feel. Work on understanding that you are not to blame—or responsible for—the thoughts, feelings, and behaviors of anyone else.

Practice the capacity to take control of your own thoughts, feelings, and actions so that you are not subject to whatever someone says or does (reacting). By choosing how and when to take responsibility for yourself, you learn the freedom of *acting*—rather than simply *reacting*—in relationships and events. For example, just because someone else is anxious around me doesn't mean that I must become anxious too (reacting). I can choose not to respond anxiously; I can remain calm and more in control of myself. That is what Jesus Christ did in many situations: when confronted or accused, he responded calmly from his own inner self, not controlled by the actions or emotions of others (Matt 12:24-28).

QUESTIONS FOR PERSONAL REFLECTION

1. What about this issue is most raising my anxiety?

2. When in the past has a similar event triggered this kind of response from me?

3. What steps have I taken in the past that have reduced my anxiety in such situations?

4. In what way do I benefit from this particular emotion?

Chapter 3

Apathy

The word "apathy" describes an absence or lack of feeling, engagement, or concern. Considered also to reflect indifference, the word implies an emptiness of emotions communicated by the two parts of the Greek language from which it is derived: "pathos," the word for feeling or passion in that language, and "a," the letter in Greek that placed before a word implies the opposite of that word, or the absence of that reality. Thus, apathy means "without emotion." At its core, the term refers to an absence of affect or at least to no noticeable display of any emotion.

You and I have known people who appear to reflect little or no emotional content in their speech or demeanor. Since all of us have been made in God's image to share a variety of emotions, the absence of any evidence of emotion suggests a learned or modified response. People who show little or no emotion possess all the emotions any of us experience but have learned to hide or disguise them for a variety of reasons. Apathy, or the withdrawal or withholding of emotions, is a practiced reaction to particular circumstances.

All of us respond with indifference to certain events, and we choose to remain emotionally aloof at particular times for specific reasons. When an absence of emotion becomes a regular response to our experiences or becomes a universal response for a prolonged period, it takes on a challenging or problematic dimension in relationships and assignments.

What Usually Generates Apathy?

When our feelings are regularly ignored, we may assume that their expression is neither wanted nor valued, and we may have chosen to suppress them. If responses or reactions to expressing emotions have involved rejection or ridicule, we may decide to keep them to ourselves.

Sometimes traumatic and extenuating negative chapters in our lives may create enough pain that we partition or separate our emotions from our conscious daily routine so that we are out of touch with their effect or appearance Sometimes we become so passionate about certain causes or issues that they take on an intensity that can control us; in order to regain a personal balance, we step back and disconnect from those issues and try to lessen the intensity of our emotions. Some people have been manipulated or abused because of their emotions, and they protect themselves by disengaging emotionally in order to be less vulnerable. A few people have never gotten beyond self-interest and self-preoccupation, and they lack the capacity to focus on a cause or become energized by an issue that does not personally benefit them.

Apathy: Biblical Encounters

Adam in the garden receiving the fruit from the tree is an example of the passive way in which someone may participate in an experience without becoming emotionally involved (Gen 3:6). A more likely model of disengagement is Jacob, who seemed oblivious to the value of his birthright when he was hungry one day and unceremoniously traded it for a bowl of lentil stew his brother had prepared (Gen 25:29-34).

Moses appeared quite removed from the plight of his Israelite brothers and sisters in Egypt when God called him from a burning bush in the wilderness to lead them out of captivity (Exod 3:11ff). His brother Aaron seemed uncommitted to God's purposes later on in the wilderness when Moses failed to return from the mountain, and he willingly shaped a golden calf for other sojourners while also planning a feast for Yahweh (Exod 32:1-8).

Were Job's companions concerned about his losses and pains, or were they mainly disconnected bystanders who offered dispassionate and useless advice (Job 4:1-7)? They sounded more like neighbors unconcerned with Job's pain than friends who had come to comfort him (Job 18:1-4; 22:1-3; 29:21-25).

The writer in Ecclesiastes appeared to alternate between interest and apathy as he described his experience with life (Eccl 4:1-6; 6:1-4). Throughout the manuscript, there is an absence of deep engagement in spite of moments when God's presence is alluded to (7:15-17).

Again, God had to deal with Jonah's apathy when God called him to deliver a message of doom to Nineveh (Jonah 1:3). The reluctant Hebrew prophet showed no interest in communicating with that Gentile city, and later he only showed displeasure that the people of the city were spared by a gracious Maker (Jonah 4:1-2). Jonah's lack of interest in carrying the message may parallel Jeremiah's first response to God when asked to speak for the Almighty. Was Jeremiah's reluctance a reflection of his fear or inadequacy, or was it a veiled attempt to disguise his indifference to Israel's plight? Born into a priestly family, he had an advantage over his Jewish brothers and sisters (Jer 1:6).

Much has been written about the innkeeper in an overcrowded Bethlehem who offered a stable overnight for an expectant Joseph and Mary. Was he an unconcerned businessman making good use of every corner in his buildings, or was he a caring stranger hoping to provide some privacy for a struggling couple? We don't know (Luke 2:7).

The stoning of Stephen in Acts 7:57-58 describes a poignant moment beyond the imminent sacrifice of that believer: the "witnesses" to his death placed their outer garments ("clothes") at the feet of a young man named Saul. Was indifference at work in the mind and heart of young Saul, causing him to stand and witness this execution, or was he already convinced by the guilt of Stephen and therefore an active player in the sacrifice? It certainly was not apathy that later prompted "threats and slaughter" from Saul when he approached the high priest for written permits to persecute the new Christian believers (Acts 9:1-2).

Practical Suggestions for Responding to Apathy

The group had gathered as a deacon body to share ideas about ministry in the months ahead. Each of them had been prompted earlier in the week to think about what they would like to see the group do to promote a sense of fellowship and nurture among members of the congregation. The deacon chair asked for ideas or suggestions on service projects or ministries they could undertake as acts of care for members or in the community. A long silence ensued. One of the deacons mentioned benevolence as a possibility for action; across the room, another deacon shared his concern that many people seeking assistance at the church door often exploited or used congregations for their personal gain and were actually not responsible enough to look for a job—or keep one.

Another extended moment of silence took place, after which someone suggested that several of the elderly church members might need a ride to church or to a doctor's appointment. After a brief pause, another deacon interjected that the people he knew in such a position were aware that they could call on anyone in the room if they had such a need.

The chairperson asked if the group was aware of any other ministry or concern to which the deacons might respond. After another moment of silence, the group decided that if no one had heard any church members mention any particular needs, then they must be doing well. Since they assumed there was no other business to attend to, the group agreed to meet again next quarter, or as needed, and shared a closing prayer. What can we learn from this group?

1. Our first response to the emotionally distant person may instruct us as to our own needs in such relationships: people who remain emotionally disconnected often become the target of others who wish to awaken emotional involvement. Beware of your own need to "fix" people who appear emotionally unattached.

2. Remember that almost all behaviors are purposeful, even if not effective: people who have positioned themselves at an emotional distance usually have done so for a reason, and unless we

understand the purpose behind the posture, we may misunderstand them.

3. Invite people who appear emotionally uninvolved to participate in selected events or relationships so as to honor their need for privacy and safety.

4. Remind yourself that your needs for inclusion and connection are not someone else's needs, and that your best approach in a relationship is to become a student of another person's uniqueness.

5. Help other people understand that grief and overextension are important experiences that require time and space from which to recover, and that some distancing may be a temporary response to particular circumstances.

6. Remember that personalities and preferences differ with each person, and some people will respond more openly to you than others.

7. Learn to understand that emotional distance in others is not a reflection of your acceptance or rejection as a person but a sign of their issue and agenda.

Dealing with Other People's Apathy

First, we may believe that we have the capacity to change someone else's point of view or behavior, but that simply is not possible. That is not to say that we should not sometimes try to persuade them of a different posture than the one they have adopted, or that we should fail to challenge them to adopt a more engaging behavior than the one they have chosen.

Second, we might take our own personal inventory to assess our own motives for wanting apathetic emotions challenged. We may have altruistic goals in mind when we wish that someone else would become more emotionally engaged or express their feelings more clearly. Perhaps we hope that they will be more clearly understood or gain a deeper satisfaction if they are more involved in a situation. On the other hand, we could discover that we are hoping they will become more vulnerable to us by engaging emotionally, or that we want to express some control over their behavior for our own benefit. By identifying our motives for wanting someone else to become more involved emotionally, we may save ourselves from inappropriate or self-serving initiatives toward them.

If we can also remember that most learned behavior is purposive, we will realize that there may be important protective reasons for the developed distance we are encountering in an apathetic response. Some people have been harmed when they risked sharing their feelings, and they have since practiced an emotional posture that protects them from further disappointment or hurt. To attempt to remove the disaffection in others without giving them an alternative way to remain emotionally safe is disarming and often frightening.

People who have adopted an emotionally disengaged posture may choose to remove it if we offer them a safe relationship in which they can express their feelings. Such reversal of thought or behavior usually occurs slowly and at the withdrawn person's pace, not ours. When years of rehearsing and establishing an emotional space have been at work, the tender and risky experience of removing that protection is gradual.

By observing people in all kinds of relationships, we can become aware of the intriguing dynamic of the ways people over- and under-function. People who tend to take initiative, be in charge, and work hard on tasks and in relationships ("over-functioners") often experience a response of lessened action, less initiative, and lower engagement by other people in a relationship ("under-functioners"). The absence of an emotional affect in certain people may occur as a response to the emotional over-engagement of someone else who is in a primary relationship with them. We have also learned that if people who over-function reduce their emotional engagement, the people who are less emotionally engaged may choose to increase their investment and emotional expression in that relationship.

Finally, we may need to come to terms with the reality that some people choose to remain withdrawn emotionally and don't plan to engage their surroundings with passion. A few people prefer a marginal posture in life, spend energy maintaining that position, and don't plan to change. Some people have concluded that emotional involvement is useless, and no effort on our part will affect that chosen position for their journey. Attempts to alter such a posture result in wasted energy.

Dealing with Our Own Apathy

Why are we withdrawn, or apathetic, ourselves? Grief and loss contribute significantly to temporary experiences of emotional withdrawal. When overcome by painful and traumatic losses, we may withdraw in order to cope with multiple emotions so that they do not overwhelm us. Sometimes we experience multiple losses when death, dreams, and even chapters in our lives are interrupted and rewritten. Recovering from significant losses takes a long time, and most of us will spend a year before we can reengage emotionally on a regular basis.

If emotional distance is accompanied by an ongoing lethargy, a different evaluation may be needed. What appears to be an emotional condition may in fact be a symptom of a medical change or situation that needs to be identified. A visit to your family doctor may help explain whether any health issues or diet deficiencies may have altered your energy level. Diabetes and iron depletions are often subtle metabolic changes that require attention. Other medical eventualities may be discovered, and a plan to counter health concerns will be in order.

When withdrawal is prolonged, we may also become preoccupied with our disconnection, especially if we have practiced a passionate or engaged lifestyle earlier. There are seasons of our souls that ebb and flow along the way, and sometimes we encounter a "winter" season when we temporarily withdraw, recoup, and then reengage. Such times may both surprise us and bother us, especially if we are not prone to plateau emotionally. Taking inventory of our joys and accomplishments during these periods may sustain us until the next attractive challenge. Though believers don't often mention them, such emotional and spiritual moratoria on the human journey are universal.

If emotional distance is an enemy to your joy, ask yourself whether you are dealing with an event or experience that has caused you anger. At times, behind some of our apathy is an angry response to a situation we dislike. Sometimes we withdraw when we are mad, and identifying possible reasons for the emotional distance may uncover strong passion underneath the apathy. Processing some of that anger, or even pain, may help release us from a marginal posture we have assumed due to our frustration.

When you wish to overcome your sense of emotional distance, begin by choosing carefully one or two causes, or one or two relationships, in which you may practice emotional engagement. Don't expect too much too quickly; be patient with yourself, and pace yourself to take a few steps at a time. If emotional closeness or passion is a new experience for you, some discomfort will take place, and your emotional safety will be at risk. Your courage and willingness to take this step is to be commended; don't rush the process.

Your apathy may have been occasioned by mistreatment or abuse. If so, you may need to spend time in pastoral counseling or therapy processing the damage and pain that others may have caused. Inappropriate behaviors leave scars that are not easily set aside, and tending to their effects may provide you some relief from an unwanted feeling of disaffection.

Whatever you do, remember that no person is born without the capacity to experience emotion. Your sense of having no feelings or showing no interest in events or relationships, apart from a neurological condition (nerve damage or disconnect), is a learned experience. It can be partly overcome over time with patience, grace, and determination. May God give you the insight and courage you need for whatever decisions are most in keeping with God's will for you!

Questions for Personal Reflection

1. What about this issue most prompts my apathy?

2. When in the past has a similar event triggered this kind of response from me?

3. What have I done before that works best when I'm feeling this way?

4. In what way do I benefit from this particular emotion?

Despair

Despair is a condition characterized by loss of hope, significant dejection, and a feeling of flatness of affect combined with a disinterest in most things. Despair emerges when an individual cannot see any viable options or solutions for her or his condition and experiences intense displeasure over a present circumstance.

Despair affects a person's outlook and perspective so that a pervasive sense of doom presides in that person's mind. Since it is coupled with a perception of limited options, despair introduces a sense of hopelessness and discouragement. The word "courage" is derived from the Latin and later French word for "heart" (*cour*), so losing courage implies literally "losing heart." People affected by such dejection usually struggle with the fear of anticipating no change or improvement in their condition, hence the emerging sense of hopelessness.

Despair and depression are "first cousins" emotionally, for a sense of hopelessness elicits a depressed state. Despair, however, is usually associated with repeated efforts or behaviors in which one fails to achieve the desired results. Depression, on the other hand, usually includes aspects of anger turned toward oneself. Medical authorities tell us that many depressive symptoms have anger as a central ingredient, while despair often does not (see, e.g., Biebel and Koenig, *New Light on Depression* [Grand Rapids: Zondervan, 2004]).

Depression also often has chemical (biological) alterations at work in the body, while despair is primarily a psychological (mental) variation. While despair usually occurs in response to a particular set of circumstances, depression is a regularly recurring emotional "low" with a more diffuse and non-specific set of originating issues.

What Usually Generates Despair?

We become desperate when we fail to achieve a desired outcome in a chosen goal, a relationship, or a plan of action. We despair when we tell ourselves that a certain accomplishment is important to us, and then we fail to achieve it after several tries. We may perceive that we have failed to arrive at it and conclude that we never will. We often become discouraged if we fail to meet our own expectations in regard to a certain measure or performance we have set as a standard for ourselves. We may compare ourselves to other people and tell ourselves that we are not succeeding as they are, which creates a pervading sense of personal inadequacy (devaluing ourselves).

When an option or particular outcome is deemed essential to our survival or happiness and we cannot meet it, we may despair. Low self-esteem may join forces with self-doubt in our minds, and we may talk ourselves into believing that we are incapable, inferior, or valueless. Loneliness and limited relationships may assault us so that we conclude that we are isolated and incapable of sustaining vital friendships. We despair when we feel that we are without resources or coping skills to overcome an overwhelming set of challenges. We may despair if we believe we cannot escape the consequences of a traumatic occurrence.

Despair: Biblical Encounters

Esau cried out in despair over missing his rightful blessing as the oldest son of Isaac, and he pled with his father for recourse (Gen 27:30-36). His bitter cry was echoed by his father, who despaired of reversing the sacred ritual he had bestowed upon Jacob.

The traveling people of Israel soon panicked of finding enough food in the wilderness, and they cried out in despair to the leader who had brought them to the desert, where they feared they would perish (Num 11:4-6). Once fed, they despaired of finding water and told Moses that they would have been better off dead than thirsty (Num 20:1-3).

More than one psalmist struggled with a despairing heart, alternating between losing hope and straining to believe again under difficult circumstances (Pss 22:1-8; 31:9-16; 38:5-13; 61:1-3; 69:1-8; etc.). This prayer book of the Jewish people is an honest and straightforward record of people captured by discouragement, hoping against hope that the God who made them had not abandoned them. Yet even the worshiper in exile who was asked to sing a song of his faith (a song of Zion) stammered and despaired of intoning a tune of hope in a foreign land (Ps 137:1-4). The writer of Ecclesiastes agreed with such hopelessness, concluding that all his own labor was pointless and that God had abandoned him (2:18-20; 3:1-6).

Was Jonah's attitude at the end of his story a temperamental reaction or a posture of despair (Jonah 4:6-9)? More than once he acted and thought impulsively, appearing to oscillate between detachment and despair.

The compassionate father of an epileptic boy brought his troubled son to Jesus' disciples for a possible healing, but his response to the Master when asked if he believed that Christ could help the boy was that of a desperate man who was close to losing all hope (Mark 9:20-24).

Several disciples of the slain Messiah, bewildered and despairing of their hope for Christ's promises and vision, returned to the ritual of their former work (fishing), though their hearts were not in it, and their spirits were deeply discouraged (John 21:1-3).

In the second epistle addressed to the church at Corinth, Paul, describing why he did not lose heart, fallible and frail though he was, spoke of having God's message of love ("this treasure") in clay tablets, so that it would be clear to all who saw him that the power available to him came from God and was not of his own doing (2 Cor 4:1-7). He then proceeded to explain that their hope in God was why he and his friends could be "afflicted in every way, but not crushed; perplexed, but not driven to despair; persecuted, but not forsaken; struck down, but not destroyed . . ." (4:8-9).

Practical Suggestions for Responding to Despair

"Don't tell me to just be patient," the man said in a low, almost inaudible voice. "It's been seven months now, and I've been looking for a job, applying here, phoning there, interviewing and hearing nothing back. Nobody wants what I do, and no one wants me to work for them. There's no window of hope anywhere. I think I'll just quit." He slumped in the chair as he said all this, and I wasn't sure whether the pause was a cue for me to say something or to wait for him to continue.

When he didn't continue, I chose to speak. "You sound discouraged. When you say 'just quit,' what are you talking about? Do you mean quit looking for work, or do you mean more than that?" I had listened to him describe his sad and discouraging job-hunting episodes several times over the past few months, but this was a new set of words he was using. Was he saying he was suicidal? I waited for his clarification.

"I'm not sure myself, Dan. I know I'm tired of feeling rejected, so I don't plan to look again for a while. Not sure what else I'm saying. I know I'm tired, just plain tired, too, and very discouraged. I don't think I can keep going on like this unless something changes . . . soon."

His voice trailed off, and I found myself asking him questions about whether he had thought of harming himself—or what other thoughts he had repeated to himself. (For his own protection, after hearing a few other discouraging words, I also recommended that he allow himself to be checked in to the safety of a hospital's care, and I called his wife and deacon to make a plan to that effect.) From talking to people like this man, I learned ways to respond to someone in despair.

1. People who despair can "infect" others with their hopelessness and discouragement. Make sure that you can manage other people's distress without joining their condition.

2. Assess your own need to help or encourage those who are in despair. Sometimes our need to heal or help another person may

exceed their desire or need to be helped. Beware of the need to "fix" other people.

3. Some people adopt a despairing attitude as a general outlook, and they will find one issue or concern after another and make despair a way of life.

4. Despairing people have lost perspective and need a listening ear that can help them regain their balance. Listening to their distress and the issues behind it constitutes a useful first assistance. Next, helping them sort out what they are actually most despairing about will help them measure the source of their discouragement so that they identify and focus on their main issues.

5. A despairing outlook often includes the myth that everything about their lives is beyond repair, when in reality one or two issues may be at the center of concern. When people mention several issues that have troubled them, a caring friend's next question can be, "Which of these is troubling you right now?" This question may help discouraged people find a place to start in regaining hope.

6. Talking about what hope they have lost—and what hope can be recovered or gained—is another way to respond redemptively to despairing emotions. You might ask, "What needs to change for you to hope that things could get better?"

7. People caught in a strong grip of despair may need medical assistance to get through their emotional valley. Ask these important questions: "Have you seen a doctor about how you are feeling?" "Are you taking any medication right now, and if so, how is it helping you?" Despair not only causes people to lose perspective and hope but also provides an opportunity for self-harm. The care of a distressed person includes assessing the power of such negative feelings. Ask, "Have you thought of harming yourself or considered taking your own life while you've felt this down?" Rather than introducing a negative thought the person didn't have before, this question gives him or her an opportunity to identify and talk about any destructive thoughts or behaviors already entertained.

Dealing with Other People's Despair

Be willing to spend time listening to the despairing thoughts and feelings of a person, but set a limit on how long you listen and how often you are available to listen. People who struggle with despair can get "stuck" in repetitive negative thinking, and they need boundaries on the reviewing of their distress. Despair can also make people unaware of the passage of time. They need help extracting themselves from negative emotions.

Observe your own response to people who share their despairing feelings often. If we listen too long or are elected too often to hear negative stories, we can begin to resent the time despairing people require of us and begin trying to avoid them. Note also that we can sometimes feel hooked into trying to argue people out of their condition or to reason with them, which rarely is useful. Despair creates what counselors sometimes call "selective inattention," which is a person's capacity to select and hear only what they expect to hear; in despair, this confirms a person's sense of hopelessness.

People captured by despair need professional care. Although friends can be good listeners, serious dejection needs medical and therapeutic attention. Resist any temptation to rescue people from despair by yourself.

The exercise of journaling or writing about despairing feelings can help people process some of their negative thoughts and emotions. The psalms collected in the Bible often record the agonizing words of a believer that found their way to written form during moments of despair. Getting someone to write about their struggles and inner pain can be a source of relief and peace of heart for them in troubled times.

Also practice asking a few questions that may assist people to reflect on the source of their despair. Such questions may give them an opportunity to regain some perspective on their loss of hope and bring relief to their distress.

Dealing with Our Own Despair

If you find yourself getting discouraged and having trouble shaking the feeling, ask yourself first if you have experienced particular changes during last few days or weeks and how they might have affected you. Also consider what you are telling yourself about issues or concerns that appear hopeless to you. As you listen to your inner conversation, try to identify messages that suggest that you can't live without a particular thing. Such myths can control our thinking and create negative, disheartening emotions.

Seek a friend or two with whom you can share the distress of feeling "down" so that you can process some of your emotional pain aloud. All of us need at least two people who will not judge or rebuke us, who listen attentively to our concerns, and whom we can trust with our honest feelings without fear of betrayal, dismissal, rejection, or ridicule. Such friends are hard to find but are essential to our emotional and spiritual well-being (many people we call "friends" in our circle of relationships are actually *acquaintances* who know us only superficially).

If your discouragement persists and seems to take control of your daily outlook, plan a visit to your doctor to determine if any medical conditions have arisen that may cause the downturn in your spirits. Hormones and chemical changes in the brain can significantly affect our daily emotional and physical responses so that we may become lethargic, morose, or unresponsive.

Also assess whether significant losses have recently taken place. Are you are processing several grief experiences at the same time? People who face multiple losses, especially suddenly (example: the death of a spouse, a move out of a home of many years, the death of a dream, and a loss of independence all at the same time) brace themselves to adjust to a variety of changes and can experience despair.

Remember that people experiencing despair have lost perspective on reality, so that your assessment of your condition is likely inaccurate. Do not trust your own "reading" of your current situation; ask for professional care to help you sort through the unrealistic dimensions of your thought process. Seek counseling. (Most of our irrational thoughts are the source of our negative feelings; if we can challenge our inaccurate and incorrect thoughts with the help of others, we can begin the process of changing our darkest emotions and reversing our deepest fears.)

Practice the biblical form of prayer that is immersed in honesty, devoid of flowery verbiage, and raw in its unrehearsed trust. The book of Psalms is a rich source of such prayers; read without pious re-editing, they reflect the faith struggle of human beings who were facing distressing days and discouraging circumstances. The practice of voicing those painful concerns was therapeutic to the psalmists, and it can be for you. Those honest prayers began with the sharing of despair and a fear of abandonment and loss of hope, and they often ended in a word of hope and eager anticipation of a better day. (Remember that many psalms were not written on one occasion but were the composite conversation of a worshiper revisiting her/his experience over time, often reflecting back.)

Require yourself to identify two positive experiences or gifts in life for every one experience that seems to be the cause of your despair. Most of us rehearse the bad over and over in our minds without pausing to contrast its presence with the good in our lives. The damage of losing perspective is that we have learned to repeat only the negative, and we should not be surprised when we inaccurately conclude that all is hopeless. Discipline yourself to focus as much on the positive as on the negative in your daily journey; such a mental exercise can reverse the impact of despair. If you are prone to forget what is good, write down what you celebrate so you can read it again whenever you feel despair.

QUESTIONS FOR PERSONAL REFLECTION

1. What am I most despairing about?

2. When in the past has a similar event triggered this kind of response from me?

3. What have I done before that works best when I'm feeling this way?

4. In what way do I benefit from this particular emotion?

Chapter 5

Doubt

Is doubt an emotion or a thought process? The capacity to question and to waiver in regard to an opinion or a judgment is first a mental activity. The fact that doubt also relates to the capacity to question beliefs, causes, and values makes it an issue that shapes our emotions. Doubt involves a thought process that questions a formerly held assumption or belief. As such, doubt engages the thinker with a set of questions connected to emotions and passions.

Doubt itself is neither positive nor negative; it may impel a person to examine faith more intently, to pursue a long-held belief more deeply, or to explore another way of seeing an issue. Doubt can also cause significant distress when a belief or cause is challenged or questioned, or when a comforting and cherished perception is under serious evaluation.

Self-doubt is the name we give to our internal questioning. Because it is related to our self-image and self-esteem, self-doubt is a devaluing of our opinions, thoughts, emotions, or perceptions. Though in rare situations it is a positive impetus to self-examination, self-doubt is usually a negative experience.

In religious circles, doubt has often been cast in a negative light. Associated with a lack of faith or considered an enemy to belief, doubt has frequently been identified with an absence of conviction or affirmation. When doubt, however, has occasioned further investigation or instigated a deeper path toward values and affirmations, it has become an ally to belief. Experiencing doubt can be significantly disconcerting to a person of faith. Questioning long-held personal affirmations and convictions has sometimes led to troubling moments for believers, whose sense of security and personal grounding can be thrown off balance or destroyed.

What Usually Generates Doubt?

Many life events can cause us to doubt. As a normal process in personal development, the transition from borrowed beliefs to personally held beliefs can often produce periods of doubt in a person's life. A traumatic experience that challenges a cherished affirmation can dislodge important foundational assumptions we hold and create stressful suspicion. A serious breach of trust with a person whose integrity or reliability we believed in can occasion bouts of doubting. Discouragement or loss of confidence can give birth to self-doubt; people who speak of "doubting God" are often experiencing significant self-doubt. An encounter with loss, suffering, or personal tragedy can dislodge a naïve and superficially cheerful attitude, leaving its victim devastated and in doubt. An inquisitive and investigative mind will employ doubt as a process of assessing assumptions and affirmations for the sake of discovering truth. Finally, a sequence of betrayal and disappointment in relationships can produce a cynicism that permeates most of life with caution and doubt.

Doubt: Biblical Encounters

When Abram and Sarah received the news that she would become pregnant and conceive a child in her older years, she laughed to herself and doubted God's message (Gen 18:9-15). When confronted by God for doubting the promise, she denied that she had doubted. The irony in this biblical visit is that the parents eventually named their son "laughter" (Isaac) in recognition of the occasion.

Was Moses doubting his own capabilities when he resisted God's call to lead the people of Israel out of Egypt, or was he doubting God's wisdom in selecting him for the job (Exod 3:7–4:2)? This future leader of the Israelites seemed torn between his doubt of a God whose name he did not know (3:13-15) and his self-doubt about his own skills in handling the assignment. Perhaps his self-imposed exile in the wilderness after his flight from Egypt had made him unsure of his safety in a land where he was wanted for killing an Egyptian (Exod 2:11-15).

Certainly the Israelites who tired of waiting for Moses to return from speaking with God and decided to make a golden calf idol were confessing their doubt of the God who had led them out of captivity (Exod 32:1-2). Their fickle allegiance to Yahweh even after several demonstrations of God's saving power is a stark reminder of how quickly we trade shallow faith for immediate relief and gratification.

Ten of the twelve spies sent by Moses to assess the condition of the promised land brought back a doubtful report to the advancing Israelites (Num 13:30-33). Only Caleb and Joshua declared that the people could conquer Canaan; the report of the majority caused widespread despair and doubt in the camp, and many of the Israelites declared that they wished they had died "on the way" (Num 14:1-4). The traveling entourage not only doubted their leaders; they also doubted the God who had called them to that journey and conquest.

While the widowed Naomi believed that she would more likely survive by returning to Israel, she also believed that God had turned against her in the loss of her husband and her two sons (Ruth 1:6-14). She doubted that God was on her side and doubted that her daughters-in-law would fair well in her own country.

Elijah's despairing journey into the desert when he ran away from Jezebel is both a picture of self-doubt and a struggle with doubting what he had believed (1 Kgs 19:2-14). His suicidal attitude drove him further away from human contact, and he wound up hiding in a cave, full of doubt, and looking for God.

The dialogue between Job and his "friends" was a curious exchange between doubting companions. Job doubted that his negative fortune was a consequence of his behavior; he also doubted that his peers understood his true situation. His friends, meanwhile, doubted that a human being suffering from so much loss could be innocent of wrongdoing (Job 17:1-16). Before the conversation ended, Job doubted God's judgment of his situation (Job 23).

The psalmists sometimes both doubted themselves and doubted their own doubts. The excruciating agony of the believer who wondered if God was listening or cared often shaped the early part of a prayer. Then the prayer ended with the psalmist's belief that the sure response of Yahweh would dispel his doubts (Pss 55; 64; 69; 74; 90:13ff, etc.).

In 2 Kings 5 Naaman, commander of an Aramean army that had taken Jewish slaves captive, tried visiting Elisha as a last resort in his search for a cure for his leprosy. When the prophet sent him to wash seven times in the Jordan River as a healing ritual, the proud commander at first rejected the instruction, doubting Elisha's judgment, the God he represented, and the efficacy of the remedy. It was the intercession of his servants that prompted Naaman to try the odd ritual that saved his life.

Thomas the disciple has long been nicknamed "Doubting Thomas" in religious and secular circles (John 20:26ff). Listed only in the Synoptic Gospels as one of the twelve who followed Jesus most closely, Thomas gained the brunt of his questioning identity in the Gospel of John, where he declared to a comforting Christ that the disciples did not know where Jesus was going when he left them (14:5). Later, he stated to his excited companions that unless he saw the "mark of the nails" and placed his hand in Christ's side, he would not believe the Messiah was alive (20:24-25).

The well-known "Great Commission" in the last chapter of the Gospel of Matthew is preceded by a short but honest phrase: "Now the eleven disciples went to Galilee, to the mountain to which Jesus had directed them. When they saw him, they worshiped him; *but some doubted*" (Matt 28:16-17).

Practical Suggestions for Responding to Doubt

"I used to believe in God, pastor, ever since I was a kid. I prayed every day for my son's safety in Iraq. When they came to tell me that he was missing in action, I held my breath . . . and my tears . . . and my hope. They never found him. About the time I was getting my legs back, my wife came down with cancer, and when the doctor told me that there wasn't a thing they could for her, I lost it. I tried praying again—just for her. I hadn't done that since I gave up on finding my boy, and then I quit. I don't know what I believe anymore . . . or if I even believe." The man choked up, pushing back tears. "I don't know if I'll ever see her again or my boy. Maybe heaven's not true either. Maybe it's all a lie."

His deep emotion and honest thought deserved my silence, so I didn't say anything in that painfully sacred moment. This man trusted me with his genuine doubt—and his small hope that maybe some of what he believed was still true. He didn't want an answer; he wanted to tell me how deep his losses were, how the people he loved could not be replaced, and how he needed time to sort out his wounded faith. I gave him a safe place to doubt.

As we see from the previous section, this man has many doubting companions in the Bible. From people like them, I have learned a few ways to respond to doubt.

1. Allow struggling believers to voice their doubts; don't stifle their expression. Listening patiently to the doubts of others communicates your openness to their concerns and your interest in their welfare.

2. The voicing of a doubt is often a search for truth and a declaration that someone wants not only to be heard but also to have his or her doubts challenged.

3. The stating of doubts can sometimes be an exercise in gaining the attention and interest of another person. In this case, it may be an invitation to a healthy debate or a deeper relationship.

4. Identifying a doubt may be a personal experience in which a person is quietly declaring that a long-held perception or belief is under serious questioning. Such an occasion is rarely helped by entering into an argument with the doubter. Instead, a gentle and interested inquiry into the nature of the question or doubt is usually far more productive and inviting.

5. Listen carefully to a voiced doubt. It may not be the main issue in a person's struggle but a way for the person to confirm your ability to listen and care.

6. Sharing a doubt can be a gesture of trust and intimacy since the doubter is allowing the listener into a more private area of tender thoughts.

7. Consider doubts as opportunities for an excursion into a deeper and more lasting faith. Doubts may be understood more as an intermediate step on a journey of faith than a final destination.

Dealing with Other People's Doubt

Respect and honor the genuine struggle of a person who is honestly examining his own beliefs and assumptions. Avoid condescending remarks. People who doubt need to give themselves permission to challenge the beliefs and values they have sometimes held dear for many years. Listen with care to the emotional content behind the words used by a person who is identifying recently developed doubts.

Mention prayer only as an aid to the person's struggle, never as a "spiritual putdown" in which you assume a superior posture to the situation. For example, you might say, "These questions are clearly causing you a great deal of concern and raising important questions about what you believe. May I pray for some peace of mind and wisdom for you as you walk through them?" By contrast, it can sound condescending and to some people to hear, "I'm going to pray for you while you're going through this period of doubt in your life, and I hope you can get past it so you can believe again."

After listening carefully, one of the first responses you can make to someone who is sharing a doubt is to ask what particular event or situation may have motivated the questions. The person's response may give you a clearer picture of what she is reacting to that may have prompted her doubts.

Lecturing or telling people what they "should" believe is not effective. Reflecting their thoughts back to them can be a more effective way to allow them to hear themselves and assess their struggles. Such feedback also conveys the message that they are being heard and taken seriously. Help doubting people remember that questioning is often a healthy exercise in the process of owning secondhand beliefs for the first time. Adolescents and young adults frequently entertain questions and doubts on their journey from a childhood faith to an affirmation of their own faith as adults. This process reflects spiritual maturity and a stronger faith foundation.

An additional dimension in maturing faith occurs when simplistic and unexamined faith formulations must withstand crises and suffering—when beliefs are tested in daily struggles. The people of Israel were asked in exile to "sing a song of Zion" for their captors, but they doubted they could sing a song of faith "in a foreign land" (Ps 137:1-4). In essence, the captives' faith was insufficient to carry them into places of suffering; they needed to refine their beliefs and build a faith that could accompany them into any challenge in life. Many Israelites grew in faith during the time of the exile.

Dealing with Our Own Doubt

Challenge your assumption that doubt is an enemy to faith, and relabel your doubts as opportunities for personal growth and faith development. Measure the amount of anxiety that raising a doubt creates within you. This will help you avoid rushing into panic-filled conclusions in order to lower the amount of your discomfort. Ask yourself, "Why does questioning this belief create so much distress for me?" Also remember that you need time to process questions and doubts. Allow yourself to reflect. Resist the temptation to conclude that any doubt you're entertaining is a conclusion you've arrived at permanently.

Make doubts about "secondhand" beliefs an invitation to explore those assumptions so that they either become your personal faith affirmations or can be set aside as borrowed axioms that carry little weight for you because you have not actually embraced or owned them. In order to be fair to the questioning process you have started, take time to question your suspicions and doubts.

Self-doubt can undermine our sense of self-worth so that we minimize our value and forget that we have been created in the image of God and are worthy in God's sight. Challenge the destructive thoughts that contaminate your self-confidence and introduce unexamined and invalid assumptions about you as a person.

Questions for Personal Reflection

1. What has caused me to feel this level of doubt?

2. When in the past has a similar event triggered this kind of response from me?

3. What have I done before that works best when I'm feeling this way?

4. In what way do I benefit from this particular emotion?

Envy

Envy is often described as a desire for an advantage possessed by another person. When we covet a skill or a possession of another person, we envy them. A response to wanting what someone else has, envy is sometimes considered to be resentment toward someone else's perceived superiority. When we envy, we begrudge someone else having something we want. Those who envy look both externally and internally: they desire something outside themselves, and they perceive themselves as lacking that particular trait or thing.

Sometimes envy is characterized as wanting and wishing to be someone other than oneself. Conversely, envy may identify an unwillingness to be oneself or a perception of inferiority by comparison with another person. That is why, though envy seems to focus on a particular possession or skill, its primary focus is on people: oneself and someone else.

What Usually Generates Envy?

We can become envious of a person we admire or look up to, especially if we compare ourselves negatively to that person. We rehearse messages of envy if we consider ourselves inferior to others. We also become envious when we have desired a particular skill or possession and discover that someone else has it. Envy can be a passionate impetus to acquire or possess a skill or trait that we aspire to as a means of improving ourselves.

Envy can become an exercise in looking outside ourselves for capacities or characteristics rather than looking internally to our own potential and gifts. When we focus on other people and what they have, we fail to investigate our own gifts and wind up coveting what other people have. The suspicion that other people have an advantage over us, or that other people have more than we have, can create an attitude that leads to envy.

Envy: Biblical Encounters

Was it envy that prompted Cain to turn on his brother Abel and kill him? Was he jealous that Yahweh had "regard" for his brother's offering and not for his own (Gen 4:2-10)? This startling Genesis episode is more than a competition between brothers to gain the favor of God. The implication is not lost: Cain wanted what Abel got (the blessing of an acceptable offering).

When Sarai learned that Hagar had been gifted with a child by Abram and she herself had not, she turned on her husband and then on the concubine she had offered to him, angry at one and envious of the other (Gen 16:2-6). Whether Hagar's attitude influenced Sarai's reaction or not, the childless wife was probably jealous of her maid's good fortune in childbearing (16:6).

Young Joseph as the object of envy by his older brothers, who, aware that he was their father's favorite child, despised him, avoided him, and eventually plotted to kill him, though they actually ended up selling him (Gen 37:2-37).

The once successful and favored King Saul displayed bouts of envy when he recognized in young David a potential competitor to his throne (1 Sam 18:6-9). Tormented by depression (and probably jealousy), Saul plotted from that time on to kill David, and he almost succeeded more than once (1 Sam 16:14-16; 19:11-14; 23:15-18).

Envy fueled Herod's anxiety when he heard of the birth of Christ, and the troubled ruler, who wanted no competition, asked the wise men to locate the child (Matt 2:1-8). When he discovered that the travelers had eluded him, he massacred all young infants born in that region, hoping to kill the child Jesus (2:16-18).

Was Martha merely complaining that Mary was not helping her with dinner when Jesus visited them, or was she envious that Mary was enjoying Christ's attention while she herself was "distracted" with many tasks (Luke 10:38-42)?

Sibling rivalry is noted several times in the Bible: between Abel and Cain, Jacob and Esau, Joseph and his brothers, Mary and Martha, and even James and John, whose mother tried to intercede for them in a petition to Jesus (Matt 20:20-23).

Religious people in Christ's day were often more of a stumbling block to him than a supportive group. Pharisees and Sadducees were jealous of his popularity (John 7:31-32) and frequently opposed his actions rather than treating him as an ally (John 9:13-24).

Practical Suggestions for Responding to Envy

"Why does everyone always call on Henry when they're looking for leadership? I've had just as many years of experience dealing with people as he has, and I have a better variety of challenges and people to work with. I wish somebody would ask me what I think or give me a chance to serve. I guess people resent the fact that I have an opinion and don't mind sharing it now and then. Can I help it if I've spent most of my adult life in the military and know how to lead people?"

Behind this man's frustration were deep feelings of being ignored and a yearning to be trusted with a position of responsibility (several of which had been given to him over the years). I wanted to reassure him that there were many places of leadership—servant-type leadership—in which he might serve during the coming year, but the challenge for this talented retired military officer was that he relished being in charge. He had trouble working with other committee members as colleagues. Whether he meant it or not, he had a high need for control in church work, and he gave other people the impression that he thought his ideas were superior to theirs. He longed to be respected by church members, but his demeanor often worked against him.

How do we respond to people who are envious? What kind of feedback can we offer?

1. People who envy are focusing on someone or something else. A useful response to them is to refocus their attention on themselves so that they can look inward instead of outward.

2. Helping people identify their concerns usually will help them focus on what they envy, which often reduces their anxiety about someone else having "more" than they have.

3. Many gifted people have spent little time examining the variety of abilities, skills, and talents they have. They need encouragement and affirmation of a person they respect who will "push" them to inquire into their own treasure of untried capacities. Ask a person struggling with envy what dreams and interests they hold as "secret interests" they have never voiced and help them voice —and try—them.

4. Remind people who are struggling with jealousy that they are spending energy on issues over which they have no control (e.g., wanting a skill someone else possesses, being someone other than themselves, wishing they had something they don't have, etc.). Such mental exercises are a poor use of energy and time.

5. Envy as a habitual mental excursion may require some pastoral counseling to dislodge the ingrained toxic thinking patterns that prevent the person from reframing their way of looking at options that can bring joy and satisfaction into his or her own life.

6. Envy and jealousy steal the joy from daily life and create feelings of frustration and inadequacy. Teach victims of envy to assess whether their attitudes and responses in life are controlled by "dead-end" mental habits like wanting to be someone else or wanting what someone else has.

7. Help release people from the illusion that they could be happy if only they possessed some unattained goal. Encourage them to refocus their lives on a goal they can attain with their own abilities.

Dealing with Other People's Envy

Remind yourself that you are not responsible for what other people covet or desire; you can only be accountable for who you are and what you can do. Avoid the perception of competing with any of your peers whenever you perceive that they are regularly comparing themselves to you in negative ways. Jealous attitudes and envious thoughts are best disarmed by humility and a sense of humor; arrogant or sarcastic responses in the face of envy only increase a charged relational atmosphere.

Where appropriate and possible, deflect comments from others about your gifts or traits by turning the content of a conversation back to them. Make the focus of the conversation no longer about you but about them—and their qualities or abilities. Affirmation and positive feedback can be an effective instrument for diffusing envy or jealousy; all of us need praise and recognition regularly, and covetousness and envy more often crowd our thoughts when affirmation is poor or absent.

Remind yourself that people who display signals of envy are quietly declaring that they think they are lacking in comparison to another person. Reacting only to their jealousy will miss their underlying struggle with feelings of inadequacy. Envy is considered one of the "seven deadly sins" in classical theological circles. When entertained repeatedly, it is a posture that can poison an individual's view of life. Help people consumed by envy to learn to examine their own gifts and talents. And, as you work with them, don't allow their jealousy to contaminate the way you see life or express your own gifts.

Dealing with Our Own Envy

Envy and jealousy are mental exercises that cause us to focus on other people's gifts first, thus robbing us of the privilege of exploring our own undiscovered capacities and traits. Ask yourself what you envy; it will help you focus on what you're struggling with and give you perspective on what you can or can't do about it. Sometimes we are jealous of others for skills they have worked hard to reach, and we are not willing to spend the time working on achieving them ourselves.

Our struggle with envy is a struggle with self-esteem. To covet another person's gifts or attainments is a declaration of our personal sense of inadequacy. It is both useful and potentially freeing to examine the messages and experiences that have given us that self-image. Low self-esteem is a devaluing of self.

The more pointed aspect of envy occurs when we desire that someone else *not* possess or have certain positive traits so that we may devalue that person. The ancients who identified envy as "deadly" were most concerned that such an outlook devalues the image of God in another person and in ourselves, and it also diminishes our capacity for community with someone else, breeding suspicion and distance instead.

Challenge the prevailing myth in our society that says the secret to happiness resides *outside* ourselves and that we are to find it either in possessing *things* or being recognized *by others* as being valuable. Rather, take the journey inward and discover your valuable talents that reflect God's image and confirm your unique value as an individual.

QUESTIONS FOR PERSONAL REFLECTION

1. Why am I dealing with this kind of doubt, and what has brought it about?

2. When in the past has a similar event triggered this kind of response from me?

3. What have I done before that works best when I'm feeling this way?

4. In what way do I benefit from this particular emotion?

Fear

Fear is an emotion generated by the perception of a specific danger to ourselves. Fear is not the same as anxiety, which appears as a generalized dread over unspecific concerns. Fear has physiological symptoms akin to anxiety: accelerated heart palpitations, perspiration, tightness of breath, muscular tension in parts of the body, and release of adrenalin and other hormones into the bloodstream.

Fear is both a physiological and an emotional response to a particular situation. Paralyzing and distressing at its extreme, fear is a reaction that alerts us to a potential harm, and thus sometimes it is also a preventive signal that assists us in avoiding a destructive situation. Fear may also be a response to an imagined danger or apprehension, since our perception of a possible threat may not be accurate.

What Usually Generates Fear?

Any perceived danger or threat to our personal safety may elicit fear. Past unpleasant or dangerous experiences often remain stored in our memory and may be reawakened by a set of similar circumstances or events in the present. Specific requirements or challenges for which we feel unprepared may stimulate fear. We may become fearful when presented with untried or new experiences. Abuse of any kind can stimulate a variety of fears, such as the fear of physical harm, the intimidation of verbal punishment, the potential trauma of sexual damage, and the threat of spiritual maltreatment. An obvious presence of danger provides an immediate sense of dread or apprehension. On the other hand, a sense of impending doom in regard to an event or change that may have catastrophic implications for our own safety, well-being, or survival can make us fearful.

Finally, an unexpected experience that throws us off balance and out of an established "comfort zone" can elicit feelings of intense fear.

Fear: Biblical Encounters

A fear of recognition (and shame?) came over the first inhabitants of the earthly garden when they heard the voice of God and realized that they had been discovered in their greed (Gen 3:9-10).

Soon after God established a covenant with Abram, the Bible says that Abram experienced a "deep and terrifying darkness" during his sleep (Gen 15:12) as God described some of the trauma and suffering that his offspring would undergo before they would be vindicated. Abram experienced a fear-filled night while struggling with the consequences of his "election" by God. Just a while later, Abram, in fear of what the king of Gerar might do to him out of attraction to Sarah, asked her to pretend to be his sister so that he would be safe while living in that land (Gen 20:1-2).

Reuben, Joseph's oldest brother, was overcome with fear when he returned to the pit where he and his brothers had left young Joseph and discovered it empty (Gen 37:29).

Was Moses' resistance to God's call that he lead Israel out of captivity actually his fear of returning to a land where he was wanted for the death of an Egyptian (Exod 3–4)?

Were the complaining Israelites on exodus from Egypt afraid of thirsting or hungering to death in the wilderness (Exod 15:34; 16:3; 17:2)?

Different psalmists acknowledged the presence and power of this universal emotion, reminding their readers of God's antidote to its effect: "Yea, though I walk through the valley of the shadow of death, I will fear no evil, for thou art with me . . ." (Ps 23:4, KJV); "The Lord is my light and my salvation; whom shall I fear? The Lord is the strength of my life, of whom shall I be afraid?" (Ps 27:1, KJV).

The promise of the Prophet Isaiah to the people of God was that when God restored them to their former place, their sorrow and their fear would be removed (Isa 14:3). Apparently the exiled people experienced both challenging emotions as they dealt with their memories and their hopes (Isa 24:17).

The young Joseph was encouraged in a dream not to give way to his fears but to receive Mary as his wife and to accept the mystery of a pregnancy he could not understand (Matt 1:20).

The disciple who asked for permission to walk on water, as the Master did, began to sink because of his fear. Jesus stretched his hand out to save Simon Peter (Matt 14:25-30). In fairness, when the disciples earlier saw Jesus himself walking on the water, they all cried out in fear (14:26).

On another occasion, experienced boatmen as they were, these same disciples, accompanied by their Master, still panicked and were overcome with fear in the face of a heavy storm (Mark 4:40-41).

The writer of 1 John recognized the power of fear as a controlling emotion and contrasted its influence with the power of God's love (1 John 4:18: "There is no fear in love, for perfect love casts out fear").

Practical Suggestions for Responding to Fear

She clutched one hand with the other as she rehearsed again what she was going to say to her boss, a "no nonsense" man who spoke with a commanding tone each time he asked her for something, a person of few words and a somewhat brittle voice. "I'm not sure I can do this," she said, sighing and holding her breath for a moment. "I'm so afraid of him—the moment he looks at me I think I'll shrink and back away and not say what I want to say. . . ."

I had encouraged her to ask for a moment to speak to her intimidating supervisor, to choose a quiet moment and use gentle words to report to him that she was so stunned by his demeanor that she could barely remember what to do to fulfill his "order." I reminded her of the option of not saying anything to him, and she shook her head at the thought of spending every work day in turmoil because of how this man delivered his directions.

Sighing one more time, she summoned her courage and asked me to remind her of the best way to approach the man, reminding me that she also feared losing her job if she brought up her concern to him. "Ask him for a moment when he a few minutes, just to share a concern that might improve how you work for him," I said. "Then, when he responds, just tell him that you are trying to learn how to work more efficiently in the office, and sometimes when he speaks to you about a request, you are so taken by the fear that you will displease him, that you are afraid you don't listen and respond as well as you might…. "Is there a way," you may ask, "for him to speak a little more softly when stating a need, so that you are not so quickly intimidated…?"

Angela's "catch" was that she was traumatized by competing fears: On the one hand, she was scared to say anything to her boss about his intimidating style; on the other, she feared each day at the office, wincing at the prospect of working daily under her ongoing dread of performing inadequately because of her reaction to this supervisor's tone and demeanor.

A few suggestions for people struggling with their fears:

1. People who are afraid need some reassurance that they will be safe around us. If you sense that someone seems to cringe or "close down" when certain people talk with them, make an extra effort to relate to them with affirmation and support. They usually fear rejection or any intense display of emotions in a conversation.

2. Help persons who are afraid to identify what they are afraid of, so that they can focus enough on the issue(s) that generate those emotions and more clearly understand the conditions under which they appear.

3. Remind people overcome by fear that they have permission to be afraid, and that no one is going to force them to confront their fears.

4. At the same time, gently remind those who are afraid of something—or someone—that not examining the dread at some time or other inevitably means repeating those fears over and over—each time the issue or situation occurs—without any hope that things can ever get "better."

5. Where possible, especially if someone has come to you to share their struggle with fear, help them assess what experience(s) in their past made them afraid (How did such fears get started? How long has the person dealt with such fears?); such reflection may help them not only identify the nature of their fear but also reduce its impact reducing its ability to exert control.

6. Help people caught up in fears to understand how much such fears control their life—and their capacity for joy—since they are often shackled by the power of their dread.

7. Invoke the value of prayer as an antidote to fears that control our life; remind the person that the psalmist asked for God's presence in the midst of his darkness ("Yea, though I walk through the valley of the shadow of death, I will *fear no evil*, for *thou art with me*, thy rod and thy staff they comfort me" [Psalm 23:4, emphasis added]).

Dealing with Other People's Fears

Make sure that people who are afraid are not in immediate danger. Help them move away physically to another place if they are traumatized by their surroundings. Ask, "Are you afraid that something is going to happen right now—or that you are in danger?"

Try to calm people who are afraid so that panic is not their first response. Get them to slow their breathing, to pace themselves so that they are not hurried, and to explain what they fear—if they can. Ask, "What do you think is most troubling you (scaring you) right now?" If they mention several things, pay attention to each, and if they pause, repeat what they have just said in order to reassure them that you are listening.

The more specific people can be about their fear, the better they can focus on what is bothering them most. Take note that fear of abuse of any kind can be traumatizing, especially if it originates from a loved one. Physical and sexual abuse are significantly disturbing, and if someone fears immediate vulnerability to one of these, help that person get to a safe environment

People who are afraid have trouble with perspective, and their capacity to listen is limited. Traumatized people also experience poor judgment and are tempted to act on limited information in order to obtain immediate relief from their distress. Help them pace themselves and "rehearse" their decisions with someone else they trust. It is important to assist them to maintain balance and not jump to inaccurate conclusions.

People who are significantly affected by their fears can grow suspicious of anyone, and in extreme situations they perceive even those who are trying to help them as working against them. Watch for signals of inordinate suspicion, which may suggest bouts of paranoia (irrational thoughts that "everyone" is after them to harm them and that therefore no one can be trusted). Such signals prompt medical attention, including hospitalization for the safety of both the individual and the community. People whose fear does not subside need the assistance of a third party—a counselor who can help them sort out their apprehensions and provide insight into ways to control the fears and curtail their power.

Speak slowly and softly to frightened people so that you neither add to their alarm nor join their intensity. Watch for your own capacity to listen patiently without succumbing to their anxiety and urgency. The compassionate listener alleviates fear by remaining calm. Engaged listening is always a gift to frightened people. Your focused presence is a calming factor when people are afraid, and encouraging them to talk about their fears gives them an increased perspective on their situation. When people's fear generates enough discomfort and anxiety to overwhelm them, affirm their right to back away and not engage their issue immediately.

Dealing with Our Own Fears

Some fears are rational and appropriate, and some fears are irrational. We can often discover the difference between the two if we slow down enough to ask, "What initiated this distress? What am I afraid of?" Sometimes our fears are connected to former experiences that traumatized us. If we can determine that there is a distant memory behind a fearful reaction, we may be able to decide whether our emotional response is due mainly to a dated event or still a present challenge.

Like worry, fear is an emotional exercise often based on worst-case scenarios or inaccurate perceptions. It is probably safe to guess that more than half of our fears do not materialize or that the thing we fear is less serious than what we've built up in our imaginations. Ask yourself, "What am I most afraid will happen?" Find a trusted friend and talk about your identified dread; the exercise of naming your fear often provides a power and perspective that tames the intimidating event so that it loses some of its control.

Respect accurate fears and plan intentional steps to avoid tackling them head on when your energy is limited or vulnerability is an issue. Some anticipated fears can be avoided and some cannot. When they cannot be avoided, try rehearsing what steps will most assist you in getting through the trauma.

When our fears begin to control our thoughts or actions to the point of steady distraction, they may take on the power of a *phobia*, which is an irrational and potent dread of certain things. Such paralyzing thoughts (obsessing) or behaviors (compulsion) require pastoral counseling, and if they interfere with our capacity to perform daily routines, we may need temporary prescribed medication. A medical doctor or a psychiatrist can become another aid to your healing if fears take on such intensity.

Some fears can be conquered. Under normal circumstances, once we have ascertained that a specific issue or event generates our apprehension, we may decide to challenge its power over us by facing it with one measured step at a time. Choosing the best situation and opportunity to counter a particular fear gives us an edge in reversing it. Choosing when, where, and to what extent to face one of our fears also gives us an advantage over frightening thoughts.

QUESTIONS FOR PERSONAL REFLECTION

1. Why am I feeling afraid?

2. When in the past has a similar event triggered this kind of response from me?

3. What have I done before that works best when I'm feeling this way?

4. In what way do I benefit from this particular emotion?

Frustration

Frustration is a state of distress in response to a perceived or real inability to reach a desired goal or an anticipated result. When we choose a valued end or projected aim, make an effort toward its realization, and fail to achieve it, we can become deeply distraught and feel stymied. The discomfort and sense of helplessness that follow our failure to reach a goal can cause significant turmoil.

Our willingness to forego, postpone, or modify our unachieved purpose can reduce frustration. Insisting on retaining our projected result in the face of defeat or circumstances beyond our control usually increases how frustrated we feel. Lack of control over hoped-for results is a major ingredient in the development and maintenance of a state of frustration.

Frustration is a learned response. Not reaching a desired objective may occasion a mild or intense emotional response, depending on the value we place on achieving our goal. The greater the anticipated hope or expended effort to achieve a given end, the greater the emotional intensity and reaction in the face of failing to achieve it. Extreme frustration can evoke a paralysis of function.

Early signs of frustration occur in children's so-called temper tantrums, when they express their displeasure at not getting what they want. Mild disappointment may give way to verbal outbursts in response to a denied request or goal, and children learn to increase the display of displeasure to the extent that their behavior may reward them with the desired aim.

What Usually Generates Frustration?

Our inability to achieve a desired result is a regular prompter of frustration. Our impatience for immediate results often triggers frustration and anger. If we have not learned to accept delayed gratification or do not understand the importance of perseverance in achieving our goals, we feel frustration. Unmet expectations affect the onset of frustration and its intensity

We are also frustrated if we believe we won't achieve our goal at all or in the way we want. Frustration is our response to not having control over an anticipated end or hope. Often underlying frustration is the suspicion that we are inadequate and therefore unable to achieve our goals.

Frustration: Biblical Encounters

Cain's violent reaction in killing his brother is preceded by his frustration that God did not accept his offering (Gen 4:5). His misplaced anger is leveled at his brother, when he is actually deeply frustrated with God (his "countenance fell"). Envy, frustration, and anger all had their say in this first biblical record of murder.

Moses, exhausted and frustrated with the overwhelming task of seeing to the physical needs of the traveling Israelites, suggested to God that his own life be terminated (Num 11:10-15). An examination of the passage suggests that the great Israelite leader was frustrated with both the people in the wilderness journey and the God who had asked him to lead them.

The tribes of Israel, distressed that most kingdoms surrounding them had a king and they themselves only had a series of judges to lead them, demanded a king for themselves through the prophet Samuel, ignoring the fact that Israel functioned without a king because God stood in that place as their supreme leader (1 Sam 8:4-22). God acceded to their demands, anticipating that they would soon find a new complaint (1 Sam 13–15).

Is there any doubt that Jonah was deeply frustrated with God for reversing a decision to destroy Nineveh on the basis of that city's repentance and genuine remorse over its sin (Jonah 4:1ff)? The pouting prophet childishly requested that God take his life, disturbed that the Maker of all people demonstrated compassion to non-Jewish believers (Jonah 4:3-5).

Micah's well-known words about what God wanted of Israel record a God disturbed over meaningless sacrifices and empty promises and seeking actions and behaviors that reflected Yahweh's higher purposes: "With what shall I come before the Lord, and bow myself before God on high . . ." (Mic 6:6-8)?

Jesus Christ himself grew weary of faithlessness and hesitancy when he encountered the weakness of a crowd, a father, and disciples in the face of a child's traumatic condition (Mark 9:19). His frustration gave way to compassion as he engaged the father's small faith and the child's misery, healing the troubled youth (Mark 9:25-27).

Practical Suggestions for Responding to Frustration

Jim listened one more time as different people raised their hands—and their objections—to his outreach plan. "This is exactly how I thought it would be again," he said to himself. "They don't want to do anything about how unfriendly we are to visitors, and they don't want anyone else to do anything about it either. No surprise. I've had it with their nitpicking resistance to anything we try. If one more person speaks up against this idea, I'm going ballistic."

His face already tense, Jim watched as the business meeting moderator recognized another raised hand for a comment on the outreach proposal. "Who is going to keep up with all these people who visit every week, and how can we be expected to visit them ourselves when we know so little about them?"

Jim bristled, looked at the questioner for a moment, then slammed his notebook onto the empty chair beside him and sat down, shaking his head. People who are frustrated like Jim have several characteristics:

1. People who experience frustration are sometimes struggling with an unidentified issue that may be bothering them more than the presented issue.

2. Frustrated people are often tired. Their energy is depleted and their perspective is lost because of fatigue.

3. People who are frustrated have often run out of options to resolve a given concern and feel defeated.

4. Frustration is usually associated with an accumulation of issues that seem to overwhelm the individual.

5. Frustrated people have often assumed personal responsibility for an outcome or solution that appears to be out of their control or reach.

6. People who become frustrated are often struggling with impatience or overextension.

7. People who expect too much of themselves or who must always "do it right" struggle with frustration.

Dealing with Other People's Frustration

A frustrated person is usually overwhelmed or distraught, and a calm verbal acknowledgment that does not increase their intensity helps the most. A "learned" response we can watch for is whether we have developed the habit of responding to frustration by sounding frustrated as well—in other words, adopting the frustrated person's intensity and demeanor. This rarely helps communication.

Listen for the person's greatest point of frustration, or help him identify it: "You sound deeply frustrated about something, Henry. Can you tell me what distresses you the most?"

Listen to your internal promptings. Are you becoming defensive or angry (perceiving yourself personally attacked)? Are you reacting to the way in which a comment is being stated, or are you responding as if you are responsible for someone else's feelings (another person's frustration)? (We are not responsible for someone else's feelings—they are).

Try to take the person's intensity seriously by acknowledging (first to yourself, if possible) that this person is frustrated because she cares about something—and she is hoping someone else will take her seriously. Ask the person to identify her frustration. Sometimes people are so overcome by their emotions that they haven't taken the time to identify what is actually upsetting them. Helping a person focus on the "main concern" will also help him gain perspective on what most is bothering him—and perhaps how to deal with it.

Don't be rushed when you ask people to share their frustration; sometimes they need time to sort out their thoughts and to name the feelings of defeat, distress, and helplessness that are often attached to frustration. Also resist the temptation to try to fix the person's situation. You will help him more if you listen attentively and then ask, "What would you like to see change in order to feel less distressed and frustrated?" In other words, give him a chance to solve his frustration first, and see what he suggests—or has tried or is willing to try.

Dealing with Our Own Frustration

We often become frustrated because we cannot control a situation or an outcome. Ask yourself what is bothering you most about a frustrating experience. We may feel overwhelmed by an accumulation of events that we do not like or that have not been resolved. The situation may seem insurmountable.

Sometimes frustration is an adult expression of the childhood "temper tantrum." We don't like what is going on, we wish the unpleasantness would disappear, or we want something to work on an immediate timetable. The bright side of frustration is that it reveals our passion for something we care about, and some frustration can become a motivating force (determination) for a stronger impetus to resolve an issue or conquer a challenge.

Voicing our frustration can also become a step toward identifying a struggle and coming to terms with our limitations and our inability to control some things in life. Acknowledging our frustrations may further assist us in disposing of the myth that we are "in charge" of all things. We need to confront the idolatry of irresponsible expectations.

The cycle of frustration, like the ebb and flow of ocean tides, has temporary intensity and then subsides for a while. Anyone wise to the cyclical power of frustration can monitor herself enough to avoid making important decisions when in the grip of an emotional reaction.

Talking with a trusted friend can help us sort out the nature and the focus of our frustrations and help us gain perspective on what is stirring inside of us. Writing about our thoughts (journaling) may also help us find boundaries to our struggle. Sharing our frustrations verbally with God—as the psalmists often did—can add dimension and insight during our distress (Pss 30; 35; 52; 69, etc).

If our frustration with anyone or anything persists over a long period, we should take note that we are choosing to dwell on it and not resolving it. Sometimes we choose to ruminate over an issue rather than resolve it, so that our aim centers on revisiting our struggle as opposed to attempting to give it closure or dispose of it.

QUESTIONS FOR PERSONAL REFLECTION
1. Why am I feeling frustrated? What frustrates me the most?

2. When in the past has a similar event triggered this kind of response from me?

3. What have I done before that works best when I'm feeling this way?

4. In what way do I benefit from this particular emotion?

Chapter 9

Guilt

Guilt is our emotional response to a thought or behavior that we believe is wrong. Characterized by regret or remorse either for having done or thought of doing something inappropriate, guilt involves mental distress in regard to a perceived trespass or infraction on our part. Often associated with sin, this emotional response follows an evaluation by us (or someone else) in which we believe we have transgressed an agreed-upon rule or law.

Guilt is a learned response. We learn from parents and other significant others to follow certain precepts or rules, and we learn that failure to observe them is a breach of contract with ourselves or someone else. The gathering and internalizing of such codes of conduct begins in early childhood, where we are said to develop a conscience, or an internal awareness of moral issues as "right or wrong." We use the word "moral" (from *mores,* or learned social customs) to describe a set of norms established by people with whom we live. Infringing upon those accepted rules or practices evokes painful emotional responses, or "pangs of conscience."

What Usually Generates Guilt?

We feel guilty when we disappoint ourselves or someone else because of something we said or did, or failed to say or do. We respond with guilt when we break our own rules of expected behaviors or have thoughts that we consider inappropriate. We learn to feel guilty if we perceive that we have offended someone or caused someone distress by virtue of a word or deed. Guilt can also be an irrational response to a perceived wrong that has no basis in reality. Often associated with remorse, guilt involves mental distress over an infraction we perceive to have committed against God. Guilt is often a reaction to our sense of personal failure in regard to keeping a moral standard to which we hold ourselves.

Guilt: Biblical Encounters

Was Cain overcome with guilt or fear when he faced the consequences of murdering his brother, Abel (Gen 4:13)? Perhaps both emotions were at work as he responded to his position as a fugitive and outcast for the rest of his life. God provided him a "safety mark" so that he would be protected, possibly itself an act of grace after some evidence of Cain's remorse in the aftermath of the tragic event.

Was guilt the silent struggle that drove Jacob to wander alone by the Jabbok brook, wrestling both with himself and God as he anticipated a meeting with the brother he betrayed and cheated (Gen 32:24)? By the early dawn, and perhaps for the rest of his life, he was left limping, a wounded but different man with a new identity and a new name. Had "the supplanter" finally confessed his guilt and embraced a different way of living?

David's irresponsible behavior with Bathsheba produced sequential guilt, identified most often in Scripture as the confessional words of Psalm 51. Responsible for placing Bathsheba's husband on the front lines in a battle so that he would be killed, then dealing both with the death of the child he and Bathsheba conceived and the ensuing consequences of his misdeed, David, according to some reports, never fully recovered from the lingering effect of his guilt (2 Sam 11–12).

Job's friends sought to identify guilt as a central dynamic in the misfortunes he encountered, while this famous victim of so much loss protested throughout the dialogues that he had committed no actions that justified his grievous punishment (Job 9).

Was Peter aware of his imperfect and irresponsible habits and struck with such guilt that he returned to his familiar work routine, yet found no "taste" even for fishing because of his guilt? (John 21).

Was not the tax collector who went to the temple to pray, in Jesus' parable, consumed by guilt as he beats his chest and says, "Got be merciful to me, a sinner!" (Luke 18:13)? Christ justifies him, in contrast to the Pharisee.

Again, one of the thieves on the cross, struggling with both his condition and his impending death, first rebukes the thief next to him by declaring that both of them are justly condemned, then pleads with the Savior who hangs beside him: "Jesus, remember me when you come in your kingly power" (Luke 23:40-42).

Was not Judas so overwhelmed by the enormous weight of his guilt for having betrayed Jesus Christ that he took his own life to "quiet" the pangs of remorse?

Paul sometimes sounded like a self-centered, overconfident apostle, but he also described himself as the "chief of sinners" when he reflected on his guilt for the suffering he had caused many people of the Way (1 Tim 1:15; Eph 3:8).

Practical Suggestions for Responding to Guilt

The man wanted to share his memory, and he asked me to listen to the story. As an employee whose job required frequent travel, he had become increasingly lonely and restless with the long, isolating nights in hotel rooms. A few years prior to our conversation, he had responded to a sexual invitation by a professional escort and had spent the night with her. Since then, he had resisted further sexual encounters, but the memory of that illicit experience and the temptation to act again on his impulse evoked significant guilt in this married father of four children. He knew he had betrayed his covenant with his wife and that he betrayed it every time he fantasized about being with another woman. His distress was obvious, and he was seeking relief by confessing. As we explored his guilt, it focused as much on the inappropriate fantasizing as it did on the sexual misbehavior of years before.

"I'm not sure I can forgive myself for betraying her," he declared, "but I also live with the guilt of inappropriate and irresponsible thoughts that I can't seem to dispel or control. I feel like a fraud in my marriage!"

There are ways to help a person riddled with guilt as this man was.

1. Listen with a keen ear for the struggle with guilt in a friend's conversation. Resist the initial temptation to dismiss a person's struggle with guilt. Take the emotion and its story seriously by acknowledging it.

2. Help the person dealing with guilt clarify the nature and the specifics of the guilt feelings so that the size and intensity of the issue may be realistically identified. A few leading questions to prompt the struggler may, in fact, reduce the perceived sense of defeat over the heaviness of the infraction.

3. Ask the guilt-ridden person how she has already "paid a price" for the wrong she identifies. Does she believe that she has "atoned" sufficiently for the misdeed? (Some people place no boundaries on their punishment for an infraction and thus live under a "life sentence" of never-ending guilt.)

3. Remember that guilt's positive contribution in people's minds is at least partially an admission that they acted wrongly. It is a reminder that they are capable of living at a higher standard.

4. Help people with guilt assess the impact of their feelings on their capacity to perform their duties. Guilt causes us not only to focus on a past issue but also distracts and preoccupies us in the present and future, consuming energy and time that could be employed to more positive use. Guilt under such power delivers double damage: it infects our memories of our past and wastes time and energy in our present.

5. When someone cannot "let go" of what happened in the past and move on, sometimes he has developed an excuse for not being able to do better. The person so consumed by guilt is sometimes actually rewarded by his "crime" because he can avoid doing what he needs to do.

6. Interpret failures, mistakes, inappropriate behavior, and random wrongs as opportunities to challenge individuals to live at a

higher level of responsibility and as an invitation to discipline themselves in order to become improved human beings.

Dealing with Other People's Guilt

People who share their guilt need a "confessor/confidant" who will receive their confession, register their pain and sorrow, and act as a witness who heard their story and acknowledged the infraction(s). Resist the temptation to offer "premature" forgiveness to a confessing person. Our need to forgive must never supersede the struggler's need to "deliver" the story without being rushed or cut short while processing the guilt.

Ask, "What troubles you most about all this?" The answer might save a listener some "wrong guessing" as to what is stressing the guilty person. A useful question further into the visit is, "In what way does your repeated 'review' of your guilt impair your capacity to function as you would like to function?" From a positive side, ask, "In what way does your reflection on your guilt provide a positive contribution to your life?"

So that you will understand more clearly what may be expected of you when someone shares her guilt with you, it may be helpful to ask, "Is there a particular reason why you have chosen to tell me this?" Or "What were you expecting/hoping I would say—or do—in response to your willingness to share this with me?" Also, in order to learn from the confessing person what he has already tried as a way of reducing his struggle, ask, "As you've struggled with this, what have you tried that has helped you sense that you are shedding some of the burden of your guilt?"

Consider any confession of guilt as an act of trust. When people share their guilt, they are often allowing themselves to be vulnerable. Receive their words as a sacred trust. Think of a set of responses or actions that will assist confessors to feel that they have come to terms with their misdeed and paid some price to atone for it (expressing remorse to an offended party, performing acts of service to atone for a transgression, writing a confession and offering it to God, etc.).

Dealing with Our Own Guilt

When guilt assails you, try to focus on specific issues or events that prompt the feelings. How legitimate is the issue? (Guilt is both appropriate and realistic or illegitimate and unrealistic.) When you can identify the source of your emotions, share them with a trusted friend or two so you can be sure the issue deserves a guilt response.

If you are dealing with someone you believe you have wronged, assess whether there is an option for reparation (repairing the damage by asking for forgiveness and perhaps reversing the injury by making amends in some appropriate way). If repair or "undoing" is not possible, work on accepting the consequences by confessing your responsibility for what happened, your remorse for the damage, and your sincere desire to atone as much as possible for the effect.

Where there is a victimized person (or persons) as a result of your actions, speak or write a confession and apology, taking responsibility for the consequences and acknowledging the part of the injury that cannot be reversed or erased. Where there is no one available to receive your confession of guilt, elect a safe and trusted person—perhaps a pastor—to hear your confession and to help you sort out what you can do to make possible amends for your error.

When your guilt is in response to failing God, seek a minister or another representative of God who can act as a "priest" to your confession and who will help you identify what actions you may take to atone for your transgression. This person will also help you understand how forgiveness and grace can restore your peace of mind.

If you are stuck with your guilt, determine if you have given yourself a "life sentence" of misery and sorrow over your sin as your perceived consequence or payment for your failure—and if that measure of compensation is appropriate to the impact of your mistake. Some guilt may never be completely erased because some actions and errors carry lifelong consequences. In such situations, practice embracing a realistic response to recurring bouts of guilt so that their occurrences do not render you incapable of functioning in a responsible way.

QUESTIONS FOR PERSONAL REFLECTION
1. Why am I feeling guilty?

2. When in the past has a similar event triggered this kind of response from me?

3. What have I done before that works best when I'm feeling this way?

4. In what way do I benefit from this particular emotion?

Chapter 10

Passion

Described as an intense desire, passion is often associated with a deeply stirring urge or appetite. The word "passion" is frequently connected to sexual fervor, and, when unbridled or inappropriate in its expression, it is identified as lust, which receives special recognition in the history of the Christian faith as one of the "seven deadly sins." People invoking a standard of higher human behavior, religious or not, have defined irresponsible passion (lust) as a self-centered impulse that "ignores the person and good of a partner" in favor of satisfying one's own sexual needs.[1] Passion is a surge of emotional responses to thoughts focused on a desire for the individual's pleasure. Self-focused satisfaction or selfish intent appears to be a key indicator of sexual passion that evolves into lust.

What Usually Generates Passion?

Repeated personal thoughts we entertain in response to a desire or interest can ignite a combination of emotions and chemical impulses in our bodies. Fervor for and a focus on personal enjoyment induces cravings for a particular issue or end. Passion is the need to express an intense or overpowering sensation that evokes pleasure and leads to personal fulfillment. When we have a physiological stirring to express sexual urges prompted by specific hormones (primarily testosterone in the male and estrogen in the female), we seek expression and relief.

Passion: Biblical Encounters

Pharaoh was overcome by passion and the desire for personal pleasure when he decided to take Sarai into his harem after Abram pretended she was his sister for his own safety (Gen 12:11-20). In that flurry of desire, Pharaoh had apparently joined several "princes" of Egypt who first reported Sarai's attractiveness to him. Like most of the men of his day, he had the view that women were primarily objects of pleasure to be manipulated by people of wealth and power.

Shechem acted out of unbridled passion and inappropriate power when he raped Dinah, Leah's daughter, and only subsequently expressed tender and loving care for her as a human being (Gen 34:1ff). The ensuing "blood revenge" enacted by two of Dinah's brothers resulted in the murder of most males in Shechem's family and led to an animosity between peoples for countless generations.

The well-known names of Sodom and Gomorrah are associated with wanton disregard for human boundaries and sexual responsibilities. The people of the town apparently were accustomed to act on their sexual impulses and satisfy their urges as desired (Gen 19:4-11). Did Lot's wife "look back" at the destroyed cities because she herself had fallen prey to uncontrolled sexual passion?

The writer of Song of Solomon was consumed with love and its passion as he shared his feelings with his reader (Song 1:1-4, 8-17). The author not only describes his love but also was clearly overtaken by the beauty of his chosen one.

Another of Jacob's children, Judah, mirrored in his sexual promiscuity the general disregard and devaluation of women in early Hebrew life (Gen 38:1-26). Passion gave way to lust and uncontrolled desire.

Perhaps the best-known incident of uncontrolled passion occurs in 2 Samuel 11 when King David noticed a neighbor's wife (Bathsheba) bathing on the roof of the house and employed his power as monarch to ask her to come to him for a sexual encounter. Remorseful later that he had committed adultery, David again used his influence first to have Bathsheba's husband Uriah return from war so that the couple's intimacy might explain a potential pregnancy. When that failed, he instructed his military leaders to have her husband placed at the "front and center" of the battle to ensure the man's death. One lustful impulse and sin led to several subsequent sins.

Several of the women who were attracted to Jesus no doubt struggled to understand a man who could love them without using them sexually. Perhaps that redemptive behavior from the Master most prompted Mary Magdalene to believe in him and follow His passion (Matt 25:55-61).

In 1 Corinthians 7:1-9, Paul addressed the reality of sexual passion by setting forth recommendations on self-control for both single and married people. Aware of the power and attraction of sexual desire, the Apostle to the Gentiles appealed to believers to set boundaries on their sexual impulses so that lust might not control their behaviors. Already in 5:1-13, Paul had underscored the importance of stopping the illicit or immoral sexual activity that was well documented in the young congregation.

Practical Suggestions for Responding to Passion

The woman slowed down a minute as we walked the path from the dining hall to the retreat recreation center and asked in a quieter voice than a minute before, "When do you think that you love someone enough and are serious enough with him to have sex with him?" We had been talking about her relationship with an older teenager, but the directness of the question surprised me. "I think that kind of intimacy is reserved for a relationship where vows and responsibilities have been exchanged," I said. "Does my answer surprise you?" She nodded at first, but then said, "No." She added, "That's what I've been taught for a long time, but I don't know . . . I feel so close to him, and I love him so much. He says he loves me, too." Her demeanor was reflective, but she was deeply engaged in the conversation. She described a bond she felt she had with him and the bewilderment of how passionate she felt when with him. "Isn't that what God wanted people to feel? Aren't we supposed to feel that way about someone we love?"

I listened to her struggle, sensing that she was confused, as many people are, between the power of physiological and emotional attraction and their relationship to "love." I eventually offered a few comments:

1. We are made in the image of God, and deep emotions of attraction and pleasure are part of the gift God has given us so that we may experience affection, care, and the joy of bonding with another person.

2. Hormonal "prompts" in our bodies are designed to elicit affection, nurture, and pleasure, even as touch is one of the senses created to communicate affection, care, nurture, pleasure, and relationship. Such promptings fuel passion but have much less to do with the enduring nature of love.

3. Passion was created to provide us pleasure and joy, but it is momentary and subject to chemical activity in the bloodstream and portions of the brain. Love as the Bible describes it in regard to the bonding experience called marriage involves a capacity to care for the welfare and value of another human being, a mutuality of relationship in which two people covenant to trust themselves to each other as to no other human being, a decision to take responsibility for the maintenance and growth of a specific person—for life—and a willingness to commit to a vow of fidelity to that person for the rest of one's life.

4. Intimacy is a gift from God for a variety of dimensions and depths of care: we can become intimate with family (*storge*), friends (*philios*), and romantic partners (*eros*). We can build intimacy with God (*agape*). There are levels of emotional, intellectual, physical, sexual, social, and spiritual intimacy that we express in appropriately deeper ways as we share a stronger bond and deeper relationship with another person.

5. We set boundaries on our levels of intimacy, which reflect the degree of commitment we share with other people. The level of sexual intimacy of sexual intercourse was designed by God to be expressed only at the highest level of commitment, which Christians identify as marriage. That is why sexual intercourse is reserved for the level of trust and commitment of marriage: apart from such, it is

a momentary physical experience leaving its participants with a false sense of closeness—and a strange sense of "connectedness"—without the benefit of a deeper joy of sharing a true, lasting connection.

Our second illustration follows: A woman called to ask if I had a few moments to talk with her in the church office, and we met a day or two later. She wore dark glasses even as she entered the pastor's office, and she only removed them when I asked her if the office lights distracted her. It was then that I noticed the swelling and bruising around her eyes. Her voice was subdued and betrayed a slight tremor as this law student began to tell me about a young lawyer whom she had dated while working as a clerk in a local attorney's office. This man had appeared at her apartment door inebriated the night before, and she had refused to unlock the door. She proceeded to tell me that he had broken the security chain of her front door, pushed his way inside, and then assaulted and raped her in her apartment.

I asked if she had called on anyone else for help. She began to cry and said she had been trapped by the offender and felt helpless to resist him. When she had tried to do so, she explained, she was struck in the face several times and told to be quiet—that she "really wanted it." I listened to her pain and sense of helplessness, along with her anger and feeling of shame for being used in such a way. We talked also about medical and safety recourses for her, and I explored what she felt she needed most in order to feel safer in her vulnerable condition. Eventually we discussed the legal issues and resources she could access and when and how she would feel ready.

Not all situations involving passion turn into lust, as the above. An involuntary sexual encounter, such as rape, is actually an action of control and violence by the perpetrator, prompted either by lust (sexual passion out of control) or destructive and deviant behaviors prompted by significant mental distortion and instability. When someone struggles with such inappropriate impulses, here are a few questions to direct the conversation:

1. Ask to what degree the person believes he has control over his desires and impulses.

2. Remind strugglers that sexual desire as passion is not a sin, since God created them both, but such passion becomes lust when we depersonalize the object of our desire in thought or action so that only *our* needs matter, or when we act on our sexual impulses with little or no regard for the other person.

3. Ask what boundaries the person has set for herself that have worked best, and what concerns or fears she may have about maintaining those boundaries.

4. When sexual passion becomes lust, remind the person that God can forgive the invasion of inappropriate ideas and that engaging in distractions from such thoughts can reduce the intensity of their immediate impact.

5. Since sexual impulses have physiological (hormonal) promptings in the body, remind the person assailed by such thoughts that physical exercise and the discipline of focusing on positive thoughts and acts of care in regard to other people can shift his interests to more appropriate concerns.

6. Help people struggling with lustful passion to remember the protective value of postponed gratification. Remind them of their capacity to set redemptive limits on their own behavior for their own good as well as for the good of others.

7. People who cannot control their passions need special attention, direction, and therapy. Provide them with such resources, or call someone who can. Of course, your moral and legal responsibilities to report anything of a criminal issue will depend on the specific nature of your relationship to the person you are counseling.

Dealing with Other People's Passion

If people confess inappropriate behavior born from passion, our most redemptive response as believers is to hear the confession without interrupting, to help them acknowledge their responsibility for any illicit action, and then to declare God's grace and forgiveness if they are struggling with not believing they can be forgiven.

A frequent misunderstanding (myth) some people hold in regard to lust is that those who experience such promptings have no control over their behavior, and are thus not responsible for their actions. We are all capable, however, of setting boundaries and controls over our passions, our sexual desires, and our physiological urges—if we choose to do so. Assess your reaction or response to irresponsible sexual behavior or passion so that you can determine if you can respond without overreacting or excessively judging the person involved. (Our two most frequent responses to lustful behavior in religious circles are either to elevate the importance of sexual transgressions as greater than all other sins, or on the other hand to pretend that such illicit behavior is of little consequence.)

Help a person who is struggling with lust to understand that sexual intercourse apart from covenants of care, respect, and mutual responsibility is actually a selfish act of self-gratification in which a partner is used for one's own satisfaction—and depersonalized in the process.

Assist the person who continues to express passion as lustful behavior to understand that God's gift of true intimacy is only found in a lasting relationship where physical and sexual intimacy are expressions of a deeper covenant between people who are committed to the care and nurture of one another through bonds (vows) of promises exchanged and kept (marriage).

Dealing with Our Own Passion

Reflect on the reality that human beings were designed by God to experience passion on many levels. Passion in and of itself is not sinful. Recognize that the internal tug-of-war between expressing the image of God and releasing our lower carnal appetites indicates our need for the Spirit of God in our lives.

Learn to distinguish between God's gift of appropriate intimacy (the nurturing and sacred closeness we experience in safe relationships) and the brief physical and sexual encounters in which we experience an emotional surge but enjoy no lasting relational connection between human beings. Instead, we focus on self-gratification without care for the partner. Remember that God has given us all the capacity for self-control and restraint so that we can establish boundaries for expressing our passion. We have the ability to channel our God-given appetites into responsible joy and intimacy.

If your sexual arousal and passion seem to control your thoughts, seek a pastor or pastoral counselor who can help you discern what you can do to find release from the oppression of obsessing over sexual desires or from self-centered behaviors that foster guilt and shame. Guard yourself from stimulants in our society that increase your preoccupation with lust and other inadequate solutions to sexual urges and behaviors. (For example, pornography advertises sexual behavior as recreational and self-satisfying, encouraging the myth that human beings find fulfillment in superficial and impersonal sexual activity.) Respect the power and attraction of sexual urges as physiological and emotional promptings that increase in adolescence and early adulthood, and avoid placing yourself in situations that lower your guard or render you more vulnerable to lustful responses to your passion.

QUESTIONS FOR PERSONAL REFLECTION

1. Why am I feeling this intense passion? Has it morphed into lust?

2. When in the past has a similar event triggered this kind of response from me?

3. What have I done before that works best when I'm feeling this way?

4. In what way do I benefit from this particular emotion?

Note

1. Rodney Hunter, ed., *Dictionary of Pastoral Care and Counseling* (Nashville: Abingdon Press, 1990) 669.

Shame

Chapter 11

The sense of having failed to live up to one's self-perception of one's image is identified as shame. Merle Fossum and Marilyn Mason described shame as the result of "the self judging the self."[1] There is a sense of deep personal humiliation at seeing ourselves as less than what we expected. This emotionally painful sensation is more than personal embarrassment; it includes a perception that we have been robbed of our dignity, self-respect, and self-image. Obviously, shame is the result of a wounded self-worth, a diminishment of our sense of value as a human being. This humiliating experience entails a perception of being exposed and vulnerable at the core of our being. Fueled by a social/relational dimension, shame is more about who we are and less about what we have done (guilt).

Self-rejection and a sense of failure as a person are characteristics of this disturbing emotion. While guilt (see chapter 9) at least offers the hope of repair and recovery, shame provides us no recourse for resolution since it is about who we *are*—not just what we did or did not do. A defeating and humbling experience, this challenging emotion requires a serious reframing of heart and mind in order for an individual to gain redemptive ground for change and hope.

What Usually Generates Shame?

We experience shame when we see ourselves as less than we wish to be. When the image we have projected for ourselves is challenged by a less attractive picture, we feel ashamed. Deep disappointment in not measuring up to an expectation we have of ourselves generates a form of self-loathing called *shame*. An experience in which we face a part of ourselves that we believe makes us a fraud to ourselves or to others stimulates a sense of shame. We experience a self-rejecting feeling that if people really knew us they would also reject us. We feel exposed and fear to be perceived as less than what others expect of us. We are afraid that we will deeply disappoint others. Shame involves a sense of losing our self-respect and wishing that we were someone better. Those who are ashamed live with a pervading suspicion that they have been weighed and found defective.

Shame: Biblical Encounters

When God asked the man and the woman in the garden where they were, they confessed that they had hidden themselves and were afraid because they were "naked." The husband and wife admitted that they suddenly felt *exposed* for who they were: people who suspected and envied God and who were weak enough to listen to the darker part of themselves (Gen 3:9-10).

The strange episode in Genesis 9:22ff reveals a scene of discomfort and shame as an inebriated father (Noah) unclothed himself and embarrassed his children. Even though the narrative was probably preserved to explain why Canaan was "cursed" as a son, the reality is that it probably also explained how one of Noah's children shamed the family name (Gen 8:22-27).

Was shame or compassion the drive force that sent Reuben to the pit where he and his brothers, in a fit of envy, had left Joseph earlier (Gen 37:29-30)?

Was the once mighty Samson not acting out of deep shame when, blinded and made to grind seed in the prison house like an animal, he called on God to give him strength to avenge his public humiliation by "bringing down the house" on the Philistines (Judg 16:28)?

The struggle between pride and shame was evident in Naaman's resistance to immersing himself in a "dirty Hebrew river" under the direction of the prophet Elisha (2 Kgs 5:1-12). The Syrian captain's servants talked him into humbling himself enough to wash in the Jordan seven times.

Peter, recognizing himself as a weak follower whose faith was fragile enough that he sank trying to walk on water and also betrayed his Lord by denying him three times, returned to his familiar routine of fishing but struggled with his sense of shame when the Master sought him (John 21:15-17).

When Paul described himself as the "chief of sinners" in one of his letters (1 Tim 1:15) and declared himself a "wretched man" for knowing that evil and sin lived inside him (Rom 7: 14-24), he was confessing that he was ashamed of himself. Though the Apostle to the Gentiles was sometimes described as a victim of pride, another part of him knew his own frailty and sinful nature.

Practical Suggestions for Responding to Shame

The woman asked to see me because she had heard me speak at a recent divorce recovery workshop in a local church, and she wanted to talk with me further about the issue of forgiveness. I had met her before, and she knew I taught at the Baptist seminary in Richmond, so we arranged to meet in my office. When she entered the office, I could see that she was burdened, and she kept looking down as she started the conversation. She began by telling me that she had been in a relationship with another Christian and had been trying to support him because he was depressed and "down on himself." She paused, and then with a quivering voice she told me that she had become intimate with him and they had shared a sexual experience. Her countenance fell again as she said this, and she looked only a moment at me, probably trying to assess my reaction. She had heard me state in a presentation that divorced people are usually vulnerable emotionally and sexually, and they need to watch for a new loneliness that might seek immediate gratification in a sexual encounter. I had warned that such an encounter would soon leave them feeling used if immediate needs were not postponed in favor of more long-term needs and compatibility.

A short moment of silence followed, at which point she told me that the experience had not brought her closer spiritually or emotionally but had done the opposite. She felt used. She also felt ashamed for having participated in the encounter and for being so "naïve." I listened, told her that I understood what she was trying to say, and advised her to watch for signs of self-anger and recrimination that might lead to self-harm. She assured me that she was not in danger of harming herself, and we talked about counseling options that would fit her need for confession, her struggle with her shame, her continued vulnerability, and the importance of not defining herself by the experience. I gave her counseling referral information and asked her to keep me posted on her welfare and her response to counseling.

Whenever you counsel a person who is dealing with shame, consider these suggestions.

1. People who carry shame have accumulated messages of self-loathing since childhood. Their willingness to share those feelings depends on their sense of trust in a conversation, their capacity to cope with their emotional baggage, and their perception of the listener's experience with grace.

2. Obviously shame is an emotionally charged issue that is difficult for anyone to broach. Respond to someone who invites you to a conversation by finding a time without distractions and a place where privacy creates confidentiality.

3. Practice the art of listening to a person's story with interest and without any appearance of judging or frowning on behaviors or thoughts. Those who feel ashamed are easily frightened or intimidated.

4. Let your first response be of clarification: "So I can understand better, tell me what bothered you most about what you just told me." The question not only assists you in focusing on the main issue in the speaker's mind but also assists that person in identifying more precisely what troubles them.

5. Acknowledge and recognize the person's trust in you as the first most valued gift in the disclosure, along with the courage the person exercised in sharing such a personal matter with you.

6. Ask the victim of shame if he can identify in what way the specific shameful issue affects his view of himself and his perception of someone else's view of him.

7. Remind anyone struggling with shame that no issue—or characteristic she possesses—is a full measure of who she is or what she is worth.

Dealing with Other People's Shame

We can only respond to other people's shame if they are willing to share about it, so practice being non-judgmental, attentive, and interested in the joys and tribulations of a neighbor. Learn also to listen to the subtle invitations people extend as opportunities to enter deeper emotional spaces in their personal lives. Many people have been ignored, misunderstood, ridiculed, or rejected enough that by the time they are adults, they are cautious about allowing others into the tender inner spaces of their psyches. Once we are early adolescents, we have learned to practice the art of self-protection in emotional places where we feel most vulnerable. We each struggle between the desire to conceal and the need to reveal our real selves.

The greatest contribution a listener can make to a person who is considering sharing her shame is to be a "safe" person, a caregiver who will not blame, criticize, judge, or add to the weight of existing shame but who will listen with interest to what may first be a tale of confession. To divulge one's shame is to tell a "secret," and the person who does so is not only courageous but also trusting. In the aftermath of having "told on themselves," some people need emotional space and distance from the person who heard their story. Interpret an attempt to secure distance after a self-revelation as self-protective behavior. We often feel embarrassed when we know someone sees our "unadorned" selves.

Help the person who experiences shame to understand that the primary positive value shame offers is the gift of seeing ourselves as fallible human beings who need the grace of Christ. It ceases to perform a redemptive (healthy) function if its lingering effect is to render us disabled or valueless. Christ came to us in our failure to release us to service and joy—aware of our limitations—not to condemn us to a worthless, valueless existence.

Ask people distressed by shame to tell what they believe about forgiveness and grace. Explain that what they believe affects how they see their shame. Can they be forgiven for whatever characteristic or issue causes them shame? In what way do they think their particular "secret fault" makes them less worthy than other fallible people—and why?

Remind people captured by shame that one of the central reasons we return to worship weekly is to "cry unto the Lord in our day of trouble" (Ps 77:1-3) on the altar of grace and to emerge each week, as we do in baptism, to "walk in newness of life" (Rom 6:4). Confession is the beginning of any struggle in worship; grace, renewal of commitment, and a brand new beginning are our next steps each first day of the week as we complete worship and leave into grace-filled service.

Dealing with Our Own Shame

The first antidote for the sickness of shame is to identify its specific source. In contrast to fear, which usually identifies a "clear and present danger," shame is often a nebulous and unclear sense of unworthiness. Sometimes the most useful first step is to ask what secret we possess that we believe makes us less worthy than others.

There is a freeing aspect to the process of "telling our secret" to a trusted person who will not add to our own debasement. Finding a "safe" person is not always easy, but it is essential. Such people can rid us of the poor perspectives we hold about ourselves. Confession as a verbal ritual can have a valuable effect on our low self-esteem, helping us name a portion of ourselves that we despise and proving that we have exercised the courage to do so.

Gestures and acts of atonement may also help us minimize the destructive effects of shame. Identifying actions or behaviors we may undertake to "pay" for our identified shame may allow us to begin processing the aspects of our life that embarrass us. At the root of our distress with shame is the persistent suspicion that we are insufficient or inadequate as people and that we can never measure up to the images we would like to portray. The struggle may be labeled *disgrace* because we are plagued by the absence of grace in our lives. The reversal of such damage is best achieved, therefore, by reframing our self-value in understanding that we are forgiven, safe, and respected by God—and by people who matter.

Reversing the damaging message of shame often involves revisiting our families of origin in which sometimes the message of disrespect was planted. If we discover that our family's disguised message to us was that we could only be forgiven if we were perfect, we may have to find another "human family" that dispels that myth (the church family?), since no one can become perfect.

In a environment in which adequacy is defined as perfection, the only redemptive alternative is to find an environment of grace. We need to surround ourselves, therefore, with carefully chosen people with whom we can believe in ourselves again—and find self-respect.

In addition, at the core of shame is the threat of broken relationships. "If you really knew who I am, you would have nothing more to do with me. You would reject me." The message of hope in contrast to that isolating possibility can only come from people we respect, from people who declare by how they treat us that our relationship with them is never in danger.

Questions for Personal Reflection

1. Over what am I feeling most ashamed?

2. When in the past has a similar event triggered this kind of response from me?

3. What have I done before that works best when I'm feeling this way?

4. In what way do I benefit from this particular emotion?

Note

1. Merle A. Fossum and Marilyn J. Mason, *Facing Shame: Families in Recovery* (New York: W. W. Norton & Co., 1986).

Sorrow

There are many aspects and dimensions to sorrow, but the most important characteristic of this emotion is sadness over loss. Made by God's design in God's image, we are people who become connected, and consequently we experience a deep sense of loss when we become disconnected. Sorrow is the sensation of missing something or someone we value. Described often as *grief*, sorrow involves an extended feeling of sadness or joylessness.

At its extreme, sorrow can become intense enough to be described as depression. As a healthy emotional response to loss, however, sorrow is a temporary reaction to missing someone (or something) to whom we attributed value and importance. Years ago, Kenneth Mitchell and Herbert Anderson identified the sorrow that affects us when we lose an important object or personal possession as "material loss."[1]

We also know sorrow when we lose a loved one, deal with a significant change, experience a limitation in redefining the self, or close dreams and chapters in our lives that have meant much to us. Sorrow is an emotional awareness that we are processing something of value that has been but no longer is. Sorrow assists us in disengaging from the past and from experiences and realities that are no longer the "way they were."

What Usually Generates Sorrow?

Any significant change involving a loss of something we have valued can cause sorrow. Possessions and material objects to which we have attached significance evoke sorrow when they are no longer present. We experience sorrow over a loss of status or position, including a modified sense of identity with a change of title, demotion, job loss, retirement, etc.

Sorrow comes to us with any loss in our capacity to function physically as we would like to, from the challenge of a physical handicap (loss of a limb, etc.), to health limitations (diabetes, heart condition, etc.). More difficult conditions such as mental issues (dementia, depression, etc.) also prompt a sense of sorrow. We know these losses are irreversible.

Sorrow emerges, too, from losses that are not always acknowledged and that sometimes are permanent. Miscarriage or abortion elicits grief; assault, rape, or other violent invasions of self register as deep sadness over loss. Some losses are ambiguous or lingering, such as a cherished dream that has not materialized for years or a projected hope (or recovery) that is always postponed and never takes place.

We also know the sorrow that comes from the loss of an important relationship. Separation from a loved one, the interruption of a significant relationship, or the loss of an important friendship can occasion deep sorrow.

We all have experienced the surge and ebb of experiences that come with sorrow over the death of a loved one: shock, numbness, anger, bouts with depression, tears, returning memories, a sense of emptiness, and the loss of joy. None of these symptoms of sorrow is usually permanent, but they can overwhelm us for a long while.

Celebrations and special events often cause both joy and sorrow, such as a family enjoying the experience of a wedding and dealing with the sorrow of a wonderful chapter in their lives that is closing in the process. New parents experience both the height of happiness in the birth of a baby and the mellow sadness of closing a significant time in their relationship as a twosome. Parents eager to send a child for a full day of school for the first time experience both the relief of a different schedule and the emptiness of a home where memories abound. People who are retiring bask in the comfort of following a less demanding schedule while also grieving the loss of structure and meaning that a job may have provided.

Sorrow: Biblical Encounters

Was God sorrowful at the change the children in the Garden of Eden were about to experience for having ignored the boundaries of creation? I believe so (Gen 3:13ff). God's response was to pronounce the creative process as full of sorrow, including the sacred act of labor (Gen 3:16, 17).

Did not Esau cry in sorrow over losing his birthright to a deceptive brother? There was agony in the imploring words he uttered to his deceived father in Genesis 27:34-36. Isaac himself "trembled very exceedingly," as the King James Version reads, suddenly aware that he had been tricked (Gen 27:33).

Years later, Jacob, now a doting father, was consumed with sorrow over the news that Joseph had apparently been killed (Gen 37:34). His grief may have lasted a long time, and some students of the Bible believe that he never fully recovered until he was stunned by the reappearance of Joseph (Gen 43:14; 45:25-28).

King David experienced deep sorrow when the child he fathered with Bathsheba lay at death's door. His appetite and sleep gone, David pleaded for the life of the infant and grieved the potential death before it actually took place. Once the child was pronounced dead, David rose, followed the funeral rituals, and then moved on (2 Sam 12:16-18, 19-23).

Job, the "poster child" for loss and suffering, spoke often of his deep sadness in the book named for him, regularly repeating the litany of losses he endured—from the death of family members to the loss of property to the loss of health and finally perhaps the loss of closeness with God. He stated more than once that his "eye is dim by reason of sorrow, and all my members are as a shadow" (Job 17:7).

The psalmist voiced in Psalm 13 the distressing sorrow of a believer who fears that he is abandoned or ignored in his sadness: "How long shall I take counsel in my soul, having sorrow in my heart daily?" (13:2). Many psalms—also called "lamentations" because they voice deep sadness—reflect the worshiper's struggle with emotions and the suspicion that God may have little sympathy for one's sorrow (Pss 5; 6; 10; 17; 28; 142; 143, and others).

Addressing the heavy oppression of the captive Israelites who longed for their home and grieved their condition, the Prophet Isaiah identified their sorrow and spoke words of hope to the people (Isa 14:3 KJV): "And it shall come to pass in the day that the Lord shall give thee rest from thy sorrow, and from thy fear, and from the hard bondage wherein thou was made to serve."

Mary and Martha both cried tears of sorrow when they greeted Jesus Christ after their brother Lazarus had died (John 11:21-35). The Messiah joined them, though we do not know exactly what led Jesus to cry that day. (Was it sorrow for the loss of a friend? Sadness at witnessing the pain of the sisters? Distress at noting their apparent lack of faith? A deep personal reflection on the power of death in this gathering?) We cannot say categorically, though perhaps he cried for several reasons.

Jesus shed heavy tears of sadness in anticipation of his own suffering and death. Pausing in his loneliness to prepare for what was to come, he shared with close friends that his soul was "exceeding sorrowful unto death" (Mark 14:34). Overcome by fatigue, and perhaps also not knowing how to care for the Teacher who had always faced each challenge calmly, the three companions fell asleep and left Jesus to his private sadness.

Bitter tears surfaced in Peter's eyes when he remembered Christ's prediction that Peter would betray him. The sorrow came from the realization that he had done exactly that (Matt 26:75). His sadness was only assuaged when the Master sought him out with other fishing disciples and symbolically reversed the effect of Peter's three denials by asking him three times if he loved him (John 21:3-17).

The Apostle Paul, often hardened by the need to speak frankly and confrontationally with churches and their members, also expressed tender sorrow at separating from congregations in which he ministered for longer periods. Leaving Ephesus, he knelt, prayed, and cried with church members as he was about to depart for Jerusalem (Acts 20:36-38). Most of those expressing their grief suspected that they would not see him alive after that visit.

The final book in the Bible describes a time when all things are made new and God's will prevails at last. Revelation 21:4 promises, "And God shall wipe away all tears from their eyes, and there shall be no more death, neither sorrow, nor crying, nor pain, neither shall there be any more pain: for the former things are passed away."

Practical Suggestions for Responding to Sorrow

The man started to say something, then shook his head the moment he felt tears coming to his eyes. He turned away, apparently embarrassed that I might see his tears, and decided to try to say something again—but choked up. Still trying to shake off the deep emotion that had overcome him, he got up from his chair and walked out of the room. He had loved his only child, his daughter, for more than twenty-one years, and he had rehearsed in his mind what one day would inevitably happen: another man would someday love her also, not as a daughter but as a woman he might marry. That day had finally come, and the anticipated grief that he would have to give her up had finally arrived for this father.

He needed time and space to collect his emotions, to sort out his feelings, and to gather his strength to accept what he had learned: the young man wanted to marry his daughter, and he knew that his daughter wanted to marry the young man. There would be time for celebration, but for the moment he had the right to shed tears that acknowledged that life provides both joy and sadness in particular moments of change.

We all face moments of change like these—some more intense and difficult than others. When you minister to someone in sorrow, remember these points:

1. Sorrow needs to be acknowledged and received, not argued against. People who love and lose need the time to grieve the reality of an important loss. They need to hear that their emotional pain is a measure of their love—and of the depth of their loss.

2. People who understand loss know that there are various experiences we share as we grieve. A sudden loss often elicits a stunning shock to the human system, and a sense of unreality and partial denial usually attends such traumatic discoveries. Allowing grievers to absorb the reality of a loss without pressing them requires care; repeating what they say as they internalize the reality may be the best response.

3. Sometimes sorrow enters a numbing and disconnecting phase when emotions and the capacity to experience the reality may be temporarily limited. You can help grieving people by interpreting their numbness as normal. Their disconnection from the moment is a sign that they are absorbing the experience to the degree that they can cope with their distressing feelings.

4. Sometimes shock and numbness scare people into believing that they have no deep feelings; reassure them that emotions will take their course, and interpret periods of depression and flatness of feeling as part of their sorrow over significant loss.

5. Some people have been taught all their lives not to display sadness or tears, and they may fight them when they appear. Reassure sorrowing people that tears and intense emotional charges are evidence of love, not feelings to be ashamed of, and that sharing them is an act of strength, not weakness.

6. When grieving people find moments (or days) of serenity, they often conclude that they are over their sad feelings and are surprised and disappointed when a new wave of intense emotions suddenly appears. Explain to people who experience such surprises that tears are part of the healing process through the journey of loss—not steps backwards from recovery.

7. Lost affection and love has a deep emotional impact on an individual, and joy is mostly absent in the ensuing weeks and months after a major loss. Sorrow takes its time, and the slow movement toward serenity, return to schedules, and basic functioning is a gradual and unexciting process. Joy will return, but only now and then, gradually, and sometimes as an unexpected companion.

Dealing with Other People's Sorrow

Help grieving people who feel embarrassed by their tears to understand that tears and sorrow are expressions of care and love. They are not shameful. Listen patiently to the story of sadness another person shares with you, and suppress the need to interject your opinion or judgment. People who choose to share feelings of sorrow need understanding and acknowledgment of their pain, not an analysis of its merit.

As mentioned before, deep sorrow results in a variety of responses, including shock, numbness, depression, outbursts of tears, guilt, anger, etc. Assist the griever to understand how normal—and temporary—these experiences are. Ask the person to identify what she misses most; one of the most helpful contributions you can make is to acknowledge the content and value of her sorrow. Resist early temptations to urge a grieving person to "move on"; such reactions are often our need to smooth over or deny the legitimate expression of emotional pain that follows a significant loss.

Assure grieving people that losing certain material objects to which we have attached symbolic value (a picture, a gift, a keepsake, etc.) causes legitimate grief and that events, artifacts, and other reminders of what we have loved and lost often prompt deep feelings of sadness.

Watch for signs that suggest that the person has gotten "stuck" in some aspect of loss. When this occurs, gently point to the possibility of his moving on in the journey of healing. (Remember, however, that most of us have the tendency to *rush* sorrow's end in order to take care of our own anxiety over having to deal with it.)

Dealing with Our Own Sorrow

Allow yourself time—and privacy, as you need it—to move through the process of loss. The sorrow we feel over loss is a measure of our love for important people and our attachment to significant issues and things. God made us to form attachments. Made in the image of God, we also grieve when we experience loss. (Behind God's anger with Israel was God's sadness at losing the relationship God wanted with the people of God.)

Seek two or three "safe" people in your circle of acquaintances, and share with them the deep emotions you feel as you slowly let go—either of a relationship, a valued experience, or a closing chapter in your life. Safe friends will not rush us through our sorrow to lower their own discomfort; they bless our stages of sadness by patiently listening.

Some people find comfort in expressing their feelings in writing, and you may want to record your thoughts and feelings during this time. Rereading what you wrote may help you identify some of the more serious aspects of your sorrow. (You need not share your written reflections with anyone else unless you want to.)

Allow yourself to be surprised by returning memories and surges of emotions that you thought were over. They are not indications that you are not healing from your sorrow but natural steps in letting go of cherished people and events in measured doses.

If you are surprised by emotions that appear in public places, give yourself permission to seek privacy until you regain your composure. Take note that some people in families have postponed their expressions of sorrow in order to take care of other people in the family circle, and you may have delayed the impact of your own emotions for days or weeks following a loss. You may then wonder why these feelings appear and are unrelated to the present moment. Delayed grievers experience a variety of postponed emotions in quieter times, when everyone else has been taken care of and no pressing requirements hinder them.

On the other hand, some of us have experienced sorrow at frequent separations and may have begun *anticipating* a loss or end of a treasured time in life, so that we experience heavy sorrow prior to an actual change or loss. (I have said goodbye to and left enough people I loved over the years that I begin to experience a deep sadness weeks before I leave a commitment or lose a treasured relationship.)

Can deep sorrow ever become an enemy? We mentioned previously that sometimes people get stuck in unhealthy places during the journey of disengagement and can't seem to move on. Watch for signals in your closure process so that you don't make an idol of any relationship, experience, or event in your life when it is time to let go of it. Speak with a pastor or counselor you trust if you sense yourself "treading water" emotionally and feel unable to get past your loss and sorrow. Those who have traveled more than a year through a significant loss can begin to assess whether they are letting go more than they are holding on. ("Getting past" does not mean having no memories of who or what was lost or expecting that any past experience or person can be "replaced"; it does mean being able to function again so that loss does not paralyze us or deprive us of living the rest of our lives.)

QUESTIONS FOR PERSONAL REFLECTION

1. Why am I grieving? What has caused my sadness?

2. When in the past has a similar event triggered this kind of response from me?

3. What have I done before that works best when I'm feeling this way?

4. In what way do I benefit from this particular emotion?

Note

1. Kenneth R. Mitchell and Herbert Anderson, *All Our Losses, All Our Griefs: Resources for Pastoral Care* (Philadelphia: Westminster Press, 1983).

Stress

Although stress is a combination of emotional responses rather than a single emotion, let's take a moment to identify its nature and its effect on people. Stress, like heat to a motor, can be positive or negative, depending on its intensity and duration. Some stress is useful in our daily routine, for it contributes focus, energy, and motivation to a given set of requirements. Students of stress call such mobilizing energy *eustress,* or positive stress. On the other hand, excessive strain and intensity, like too much heat to a motor, can reduce positive aspects of the pressure. When such intensity occurs, human effort can be rendered less useful, and the individual loses the capacity to function effectively. We call such negative pressure *distress,* or debilitating stress.

Combining physiological and emotional symptoms, stress is our response to requirements that challenge our capacity to cope in a given situation. Physiological characteristics include an increased heart rate, perspiration of the hands, accelerated breathing, and an increased muscular tension in the body. Glandular activity under stress includes the secretion of epinephrine and cortisol, eventually resulting in a decreased capacity to process thoughts and maintain clear judgment.[1] Such cases of excessive stress result in a sense of helplessness and incapacity to function adequately in the daily routine.

Although stress is not a single emotion, it causes anxiety, distress, fear, panic, and emotional suffering. Ministers and other caregivers increasingly face the need to respond to parishioners who are oppressed by this controlling and complex phenomenon.

What Usually Generates Stress?

Any significant change can produce stress, and most of us are juggling several changes at once. Thomas Holmes and other physicians who have studied the effects of stress on the human body and psyche tells us that certain changes affect us physiologically and emotionally more than others.[2] Death triggers the heaviest stress in our life, and the death of a child, regardless of age, delivers the hardest blow. The death of a spouse affords almost as much distress, but the impact of losing a child is the greatest.

Other stressors include divorce, the death of other family members or a close friend, and significant life-changing events such as a marriage, retirement, debilitating accident, incarceration, or the loss of a job. Of course, there are other stressors, such as pregnancy or miscarriage, assuming a house mortgage, financial setback, a geographic move, and illness (physical or mental).

Stress increases when a family member leaves home, a child starts school, a spouse takes on or quits a job, or family conflicts escalate.

Most of us deal with a variety of changes at the same time, and the convergence of stressful experiences at the same time over a period of several months can overwhelm us.

Stress: Biblical Encounters

The book of Job and its central figure emerge as the Old Testament's premier example of multiple issues converging to produce unparalleled stress. The loss of family members, the loss of property, the loss of health, and the loss of spiritual security all combined to make Job the epitome of a stressed human being at his limit. Job's arguments with his "friends" illustrate the intensity of his distress, and the entire book documents the reality of his layered physical, emotional, and spiritual misery.

Joseph, husband to Mary, faced a growing set of stressors while anticipating a marriage with his betrothed: (1) he discovered that his wife-to-be was pregnant, and under the law she could be stoned as punishment; (2) he was told to leave his home in order to register for the census (Nazareth to Bethlehem) and then was told not to return; (3) he fled his country with Mary and the baby to avoid the child's death, landing in Egypt, a country where Jewish families were often not well received; (4) he was responsible for a mother and child while temporarily unemployed; and (5) he returned to family and Israelites whose male children under two years of age had been hunted down and killed

The ordeal of Jesus Christ in Gethsemane records his deep sense of isolation, his anticipated experience with death, his disappointment with friends, his change of status from "sought after" to "sought/wanted," his emotional trauma—to the point of sweating drops of blood—and his telling those close by that his "soul is exceeding sorrowful, even unto death" (Matt 26:37-38).

Practical Suggestions for Responding to Stress

He walked into the classroom to take his midterm test, sat down, placed his head on the table, then raised his eyes, and beckoned to me to leave the room with him for a moment. "My wife and I are expecting, as you know, and she's apparently in labor...or wondering if she is. . . . The church cantata is scheduled for this weekend, and I . . . ." He stopped, caught his breath, then added, "I've not had a chance to read the material, and I know I'll flunk this test if I take it now." Then, lowering his head and dropping his gaze, he added further, "I'm also supposed to graduate in three weeks, and I can't afford not to take this test. What do I do?" It was a partly a question, partly a plea for help. He also had not slept the night before.

I placed my hand on his shoulder, slightly, and told him to go home—and call, on his way—to make sure how his wife was—and what she needed. I told him to "go be a father," to check if anyone else could lead the choir rehearsal that week, and to forget about the test for the time being. He could call me in a week or two and take the test when he was ready, before graduation, and I would give it to him when he could focus. After I asked him if there was any other professor he needed to "get a word to," I asked him if he was settled enough to drive home—or if he needed someone else to drive him to his wife. (He had calmed down by then and said he could drive.) I suggested that he take two or three minutes to focus and let us know if he still felt able to drive.

Stress can render us perplexed at best—and even paralyzed and overwhelmed. These tips can help you or someone who seeks your counsel deal with stress:

1. Take notice of physiological signals that indicate stress. Shortness of breath, sweaty palms, increased heart rate, dry mouth, and a general agitation warn us that we are facing our limit. Note also some of the emotional signs of stress: heightened anxiety, agitation, preoccupation and distraction, impaired judgment, tendency to panic, etc.

2. Introduce relaxation exercises to help calm the agitation and distress that distract you. (Breathe in and out slowly, close your eyes and meditate on a peace-filled moment, relax tense muscles by massaging them and letting go of the tension; do the same for your jaw) neck, and limbs. Pray for your mind, your emotions, and your heart. Get a massage; take a long walk. Pay attention to nature.

3. Harness your runaway thoughts by asking yourself what is most worrying you or controlling you. When you have identified one, two, or three primary concerns, ask yourself which one you need to work on first, including the amount of control you actually have over whether it will occur or not.

4. Ask yourself what part of your stress is ruled by your expectations about certain outcomes and schedules; then ask yourself why you require such strong control over things—and what would happen if you didn't try to control them.

5. If you feel overwhelmed, assess what issues or deadlines are less important and can be renegotiated. Remind yourself that some of your self-imposed deadlines and expectations were set *before* the intrusion or surprise of additional requirements. Give yourself permission to renegotiate.

6. Revisit the reality that all of us live by grace, that we are fallible human beings, and that wisdom and good judgment trump inflexibility and obsessions.

Dealing with Other People's Stress

1. Recognize that stressed people who engage you are affected by deep anxiety and overextension and therefore incapable of hearing well, responding logically at first, or managing stressful responses to their stress.

2. Help stressed persons by not taking on their intensity or agitation, but by inviting them calmly to "catch their breath," slow down, and identify their points of greatest felt pressure, so that they can sort out what most needs attention first.

3. As possible, assist the stressed person to consider that some of the pressure they are feeling may be created by their own expectations, often excessive or unrealistic.

4. Remind the person struggling with pressure that one of the actions they can take first in response to stress is to begin to make distinctions between what is important (but not urgent), what is important and urgent, and what may be neither important nor urgent. Sometimes we create artificial deadlines, imaginary urgencies, and accelerated schedules that the issue at hand does not demand.

5. Following the advice of folks who care for people experiencing stress, ask the stressed person to ask themselves, "Is the issue(s) over which I'm struggling worth the amount of energy and strain I'm currently expending on it?" (The writer remembers fuming for over thirty minutes over a bottle he broke—which $6 subsequently replaced.)

6. Help the stressed person to "take time out" to gain control of the intense emotions that have built up so that they may pace themselves, slow down to gain a better perspective of their issue(s), and regain a balance lost in the heat of the moment. Suggest that they sit down, begin to breathe deeply and more slowly, and begin to tell themselves what has generated the "alarm" they are experiencing.

7. Assist those who are experiencing significant strain to ask themselves what specific messages they are repeating to themselves at the time. We have collected a number of "scripts" from childhood that we tend to "play" like a recording when under duress. For example: "I can't handle all this," or "I can't change any of this," and "I can't take this any longer," or "This is all hopeless," and "I have to do all of this myself," etc.

8. Remind stressed people that some degree of stress is like heat to a motor. Stress creates motivation and engagement, but only up to a point; it is in excess that stress is an enemy to health—and hope.

9. Teach stressed people what Jesus Christ knew—that prayer is an antidote to stress and heaviness of thought, and that time to pray at the end of the day—or at the place of greatest need—has a calming and healing effect on our tendency to panic under pressure. Pray for God's peace of mind, discernment, and perspective over matters which distress us.

Dealing with Our Own Stress

1. Learn your own warning signs that stress is about to overwhelm you: Am I more irritable than usual? Are my responses to people sharp—and "pointed"? Do I have recurring headaches that slow my capacity to focus? Am I sleepy, fatigued? Have I lost my appetite—or am I eating more than usual, for comfort sake? Is my sleep interrupted, uneven, controlled by insomnia (or am I sleeping excessively, reluctant to "get up and go")? Is my judgment impaired, so that I'm making poor decisions? Am I so preoccupied that I can't seem to function properly at work or home? These and other signs of excessive stress are warnings that I need to slow down and deal with the weight of harmful pressure in my life.

2. When stressed, if I can ask myself—and identify—"What is causing all this consternation?" or "What am I stressing over?" I have a better chance of gaining some control over my reactions, since clarifying the nature of the stress often reduces its impact and size (it looks and sounds more manageable when I "name" it).

3. Listen to the internal voices that keep repeating defeating and often inaccurate messages to yourself—and challenge those negative thoughts: "I can't make it" (How do you know?), "It's hopeless" (What is hopeless?), "It's all over" (What is all over, and what evidence do I have that everything is over?), "I have to do it all right now" (Why must everything be done immediately?).

4. Since you have control over your thoughts and your pace (rhythm), learn to pace yourself by slowing down, breathing deeper and slower, so that you reduce the physiological and emotional tempo that adds to your frenzy; take "time out" so that you can assess your actual circumstances and regain your perspective.

5. Once you have identified the issues or concerns that appear to have triggered your stress, try asking yourself a couple of helpful questions that can affect the measure of your intensity: (a) How important is this issue? (b) Is this issue both important *and* urgent? (c) Is it important but not urgent? (Sometimes we create our own urgency). Prioritize your challenges: it will reduce your stress and help you focus on what to work on first.

6. Ask yourself, "What can I do about what I'm stressing over? In what way can I affect what is bothering me?" (If it's beyond my control, what am I gaining by worrying about it? Many of the things we brood over never take place.)

7. Activate your prayer experience by asking God to give you clarity, perspective, and discernment.

QUESTIONS FOR PERSONAL REFLECTION

1. Why am I feeling so much stress?

2. When in the past has a similar event triggered this kind of response from me?

3. What have I done before that works best when I'm feeling this way?

4. In what way do I benefit from this particular emotion?

Notes

1. Paul J. Peterson, "Stress and Stress Management," in *Dictionary of Pastoral Care & Counseling*, ed. Rodney J. Hunter (Nashville: Abingdon: 1990).

2. See, for example, Thomas H. Holmes and Richard H. Rahe, "The Social Readjustment Rating Scale," *Journal of Psychosomatic Research* 11/2 (August 1967): 213–18. See also "The Holmes and Rahe Stress Scale: Understanding the Impact of Long-term Stress," http://www.mindtools.com/pages/article/newTCS_82.htm (accessed 29 December 2011).

Chapter 14

Suspicion

Suspicion is a feeling of distrust in regard to someone or something. It is grounded on the persistent concern that something is not as it appears to be. Imagining that what is said to us is not accurate triggers a response of caution and doubt that affects how we relate to another person. Because such responses are accompanied by a specific set of emotional experiences, we will explore what some people call the "feeling" of suspicion.

Some people have grown up in an environment in which they have been deceived by someone they trusted. Repeated experiences of such deception teach us to distrust others and to address most relationships from a position of caution and ambivalence. The suspicious person anticipates or expects that an agenda is purposely hidden in a conversation or a relationship. People who approach relationships with distrust and significant caution relate to others out of a sense of suspicion rather than trust.

What Usually Generates Suspicion?

Some people want more privacy than others and prefer the company of fewer people. The so-called "introvert" (in what is popularly known as the Myers-Briggs Personality Type inventory) is a person who gains more personal energy from working in a solitary environment. That characteristic means such persons expend (lose) energy in relational activity, while so-called "extroverts" tend to become energized by the presence of and contact with other human beings, and they lose energy more often in solitude or quiet.

Some people are "shy" in personal encounters and prefer quieter relational experiences. Such people, like the introvert, are not necessarily suspicious or distrustful of relationships; they simply like one-on-one conversations and relationships that neither intimidate nor overwhelm. These personality differences are neither good nor bad, for each unique personality has strengths and weaknesses. By contrast to the introvert or the shy person, the person who relates out of suspicion has learned this posture in reaction to certain negative experiences with other people. How does that happen?

People who experience accentuated caution in relationships have usually been deceived by significant people during the formative years. Having trusted and become vulnerable to people important to their survival, distrustful people feel betrayed and want to protect themselves from being hurt again.

Deceived people experience a sense of safety and comfort when creating an emotional "space" between others and themselves. If we have been deceived by people close to us, we react by protecting ourselves because we know our vulnerability—and the pain that comes with betrayal.

Cautious and distrusting people often conclude that most people work out of "hidden agendas" in relationships, so that people are rarely what they seem to be and most people *work* relationships to meet their own needs.

Behind the cautionary distance and emotional space some people create for themselves often lies an unacknowledged awareness of their vulnerability and a deep disdain for it—as a perceived weakness in themselves and in human relationships.

Suspicion: Biblical Encounters

One of the first "dialogues" in Genesis portrays the serpent in the Garden of Eden planting the first seeds of suspicion in its inhabitants: "Has God indeed said . . . ? . . . God knows that in the day you eat of it [the fruit] your eyes will be opened and you will be like God . . ." (Gen 3:1b, 5) Suspicion about God's intent in setting boundaries in the created world occasioned the first pangs of dissension and distance between the creatures and their Creator.

When Moses delayed in returning to the traveling Israelites on the road to the promised land, the people below the mountain began to suspect that God had abandoned them, and they urged

Aaron to make another god to see them through the wilderness (Exod 32:1).

Did Job suspect that God had abandoned him when he railed against the many calamities that had befallen him (Job 7)? Several sections of the book's recorded arguments suggest a serious struggle between suspecting that God had forgotten him and hesitantly reaffirming his faith that God would vindicate him.

Did Naaman suspect that Elisha was trying to make a fool of the Syrian military leader by telling him to dip in the dirty Jordan seven times in order to be cured of his malady (2 Kings 5)? The Damascus officer was suspicious of the prophet's motivation.

Several psalmists voiced a deep suspicion that God either did not care about their plight or had abandoned them in their time of need (Pss 6; 10; 13; 22; 28; 38; 42, etc.).

Isaiah suspected *himself* of being inadequate (Isa 6:5) when he experienced the presence of a "holy Other" in the temple who called him during an encounter in worship to carry a message to Israel.

Herod's suspicion that the newborn Jesus had come into his part of the world to supplant him as king of Judea prompted him to ask the visiting wise men to report the baby's whereabouts so that he could have him killed (Matt 2:8, 16). (Herod's fear and reaction were not surprising given what he thought he had to lose with a new "king" around—but why was "all of Jerusalem" troubled with him? [Matt 2:3])

The best and worst of one of Jesus Christ's days is recorded in the Fourth Gospel when the Master healed a man blind from birth and then had to deal with the stubborn suspicion of religious leaders who would rather question the miraculous cure than consider it as evidence that God was in their midst (John 9:18-34).

Saul (later Paul) and many other orthodox Jews were suspicious enough of the "new religion" that they devoted themselves to killing its followers. Stephen was just one of the followers of the Way who was stoned to death, the first execution of a believer recorded in the book of Acts (7:54-60).

The young and naïve church members in Galatia were easily swept off their spiritual feet by legalists who persuaded them to suspect Paul, his calling, and his teaching (Gal 3:1ff). The Apostle to the Gentiles spent at least half of his letter to the Galatians trying to reduce the pernicious distrust of him that a small group of Judaizers had planted in their minds.

Practical Suggestions for Responding to Suspicion

The man answered the phone when I called this time (I had left a message that I hoped to visit him at home at his convenience), and when I told him I was hoping to plan a time when I could see him, he replied, "And what's the nature of your visit?" I responded that the deacons were undertaking a self-evaluation of our church to learn from church members who had at one time been active in church participation but no longer were. We wanted to learn how we could improve our relationship with church members so that we would not fail to care for them—as apparently we might have failed in our relationship with him and his family.

"I'm not sure any conversation we would have would be of much use to you, pastor," the man said. "We left the church because we no longer agree with the direction it's taking, and that's all. We need to go where we fit better, and if the majority of the church wants to go in another direction, then we need to go our separate ways."

"I can appreciate that," I said, "and clarifying any differences of vision or emphasis would help us as we prayerfully assess what those differences are. We could learn from you if we could listen to what you think is missing—or what direction you think we should go—so we can assess if we are truly at different places in God's work. Would that be possible?"

"I think we are pretty clear about where we see ourselves, and the church has made clear where it wants to go, and I doubt it would do much good to go over it again. We simply don't want to do that. Thanks for calling, and we wish you well, and we'll find where God wants us to work next. Thanks."

1. A suspicious atmosphere like the one created between this man and our church requires space for self-protection and preservation. Allow suspecting people to maintain emotional and physical distance if they need to.

2. Clarity of purpose reduces the anxiety of a hidden intent in a conversation with a suspicious person. The clearer we are with what we want, the less room we allow for misunderstanding. Distrusting emotions respond better to brevity and clarity in a relationship.

3. People who struggle with suspicion need the freedom to choose those with whom they want to share confidences. We may offer our friendship or trust, but cautious people will deposit trust in those whom they alone select.

4. As much as possible, allow distrustful people to take initiative toward you instead of taking initiative toward them in regard to inquiries or concerns you may have. (Folks who suspect others of possessing an agenda behind the questions they ask feel more secure when they are the ones inquiring or exploring an issue.)

5. Respond to questions and concerns a distrustful person makes in a direct and concise manner.

6. Remember that people who suspect others often have a history of betrayal, deceit, or inconsistent relationships from significant others, and their distrust of you is not personal. They keep most people at a distance.

7. Take note that people struggling with suspicion have arrived at that position because of challenging experiences with trust in their past, and, if they choose to trust you, consider their decision to do so a sacred act.

Dealing with Other People's Suspicion

Allow distrustful people to maintain their needed emotional space in a conversation. Resist the temptation to probe any issue without their permission, which usually occurs with a straightforward comment they decide to share. Remember that people who have learned to distrust are usually suspicious of unclear relationships or undefined expectations. Practice being clear, concise, and up front with your responses or initiatives.

Speak for yourself when expressing an opinion or response about any issue, refraining from the perception that you "know" or "understand" how a suspecting person thinks or feels. Ask if you can be of support in specific ways, and let a person struggling with suspicion indicate what she allows you to do for her rather than offering your own suggestions about what you might do.

Express care and interest if you are aware of a crisis or issue in the person's life that is common knowledge to the church or community, but refrain from asking questions about private, undisclosed matters or an issue you may have heard about indirectly.

People who feel deceived or betrayed by someone in their past may respond to you cautiously or with suspicion, but you are not responsible for their distrust, and their suspicion is not a result of your actions in the relationship.

Distrusting people rarely have more than one or two friends at a level of significant trust; don't make it your goal to win their friendship. Instead, focus on being a trustworthy listener.

Dealing with Our Own Suspicion

Take note of your sense of how you approach relationships. Do you assume some level of trust, no trust at all, or too much trust? Knowing how we begin in relationships may help us understand our emotional history and recognize how we tend to respond to relational invitations. Cautious signals often indicate that we have sometimes been excessively trusting (gullible) and have learned to protect ourselves in order not to feel vulnerable.

Deceived and betrayed individuals need one or two safe relationships (with people we can trust implicitly) so that we don't isolate ourselves. In order to renew some sense of trust and safety in human relationships, choose a friend or two carefully and intentionally from your circle of acquaintances over the years.

Some suspicious people struggle with friendships or with the desire to marry, debating whether they can ever trust someone enough to assume that level of confidence in a relationship. Check to see if your past suspicions are affecting the dreams and hopes you've entertained over the years.

Some people have learned to sense the world as a suspicious place because they grew up in manipulative relationships with people who harmed them emotionally or used them in order to fulfill their own expectations. The caution that results from such experiences is not surprising, especially if the people who manipulated them were adults significant to their survival.

Some degree of caution and suspicion in relationships may be appropriate, particularly in a society that appears to practice increased impersonal and self-serving behaviors.[1] If overcoming what you assess as "excessive" suspicion is your goal, speak with a pastoral counselor or a therapist who can help you identify what you would like to modify about your emotional responses in relationships. We can change how we feel by addressing the thoughts and messages that have shaped our reactions to people and events.[2]

Questions for Personal Reflection

1. Why am I feeling so much suspicion?

2. When in the past has a similar event triggered this kind of response from me?

3. What have I done before that works best when I'm feeling this way?

4. In what way do I benefit from this particular emotion?

Notes

1. See Nina Brown's *Children of the Self-Absorbed* (Oakland CA: New Harbinger, 2001).

2. See Patricia Rushford, *The Jack & Jill Syndrome (Healing for Broken Children)* (Grand Rapids MI: Fleming Revell, 1996).

Other available titles from SMYTH & HELWYS

Beyond the American Dream
Millard Fuller

In 1968, Millard finished the story of his journey from pauper to millionaire to home builder. His wife, Linda, occasionally would ask him about getting it published, but Millard would reply, "Not now. I'm too busy." This is that story.   978-1-57312-563-5   272 pages/pb   **$20.00**

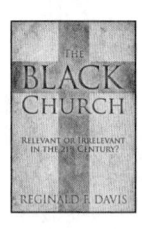

The Black Church
Relevant or Irrelevant in the 21st Century?
Reginald F. Davis

The Black Church contends that a relevant church struggles to correct oppression, not maintain it. How can the black church focus on the liberation of the black community, thereby reclaiming the loyalty and respect of the black community?   978-1-57312-557-4   144 pages/pb   **$15.00**

Blissful Affliction
The Ministry and Misery of Writing
Judson Edwards

Edwards draws from more than forty years of writing experience to explore why we use the written word to change lives and how to improve the writing craft.   978-1-57312-594-9   144 pages/pb   **$15.00**

Bottom Line Beliefs
Twelve Doctrines All Christians Hold in Common (Sort of)
Michael B. Brown

Despite our differences, there are principles that are bedrock to the Christian faith. These are the subject of Michael Brown's *Bottom Line Beliefs*.   978-1-57312-520-8   112 pages/pb   **$15.00**

Christian Civility in an Uncivil World
Mitch Carnell, ed.

When we encounter a Christian who thinks and believes differently, we often experience that difference as an attack on the principles upon which we have built our lives and as a betrayal to the faith. However, it is possible for Christians to retain their differences and yet unite in respect for each other. It is possible to love one another and at the same time retain our individual beliefs.   978-1-57312-537-6   160 pages/pb   **$17.00**

To order call 1-800-747-3016 or visit www.helwys.com

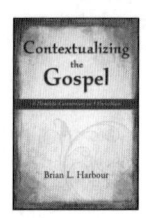

Contextualizing the Gospel
A Homiletic Commentary on 1 Corinthians

Brian L. Harbour

Harbour examines every part of Paul's letter, providing a rich resource for those who want to struggle with the difficult texts as well as the simple texts, who want to know how God's word—all of it—intersects with their lives today.

978-1-57312-589-5   240 pages/pb   **$19.00**

The Disturbing Galilean
Essays About Jesus

Malcolm Tolbert

In this captivating collection of essays, Dr. Malcolm Tolbert reflects on nearly two dozen stories taken largely from the Synoptic Gospels. Those stories range from Jesus' birth, temptation, teaching, anguish at Gethsemane, and crucifixion.

978-1-57312-530-7   140 pages/pb   **$15.00**

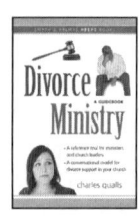

Divorce Ministry
A Guidebook

Charles Qualls

This book shares with the reader the value of establishing a divorce recovery ministry while also offering practical insights on establishing your own unique church-affiliated program. Whether you are working individually with one divorced person or leading a large group, *Divorce Ministry: A Guidebook* provides helpful resources to guide you through the emotional and relational issues divorced people often encounter.

978-1-57312-588-8   156 pages/pb   **$16.00**

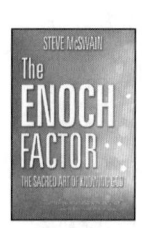

The Enoch Factor
The Sacred Art of Knowing God

Stephen McSwain

The Enoch Factor is a persuasive argument for a more enlightened religious dialogue in America, one that affirms the goals of all religions—guiding followers in self-awareness, finding serenity and happiness, and discovering what the author describes as "the sacred art of knowing God."

978-1-57312-556-7   256 pages/pb   **$21.00**

To order call 1-800-747-3016 or visit **www.helwys.com**

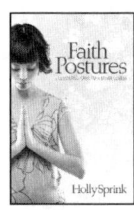

Faith Postures
Cultivating Christian Mindfulness
Holly Sprink

Sprink guides readers through her own growing awareness of God's desire for relationship and of developing the emotional, physical, spiritual postures that enable us to learn to be still, to listen, to be mindful of the One outside ourselves. 1-978-57312-547-5 160 pages/pb **$16.00**

The Good News According to Jesus
A New Kind of Christianity for a New Kind of Christian
Chuck Queen

In *The Good News According to Jesus*, Chuck Queen contends that when we broaden our study of Jesus, the result is a richer, deeper, healthier, more relevant and holistic gospel, a Christianity that can transform this world into God's new world.

978-1-57312-528-4 216 pages/pb **$18.00**

Healing Our Hurts
Coping with Difficult Emotions
Daniel Bagby

In *Healing Our Hurts*, Daniel Bagby identifies and explains all the dynamics at play in these complex emotions. Offering practical biblical insights to these feelings, he interprets faith-based responses to separate overly religious piety from true, natural human emotion. This book helps us learn how to deal with life's difficult emotions in a redemptive and responsible way. 978-1-57312-613-7 144 pages/pb **$15.00**

Hope for the Thinking Christian
Seeking a Path of Faith through Everyday Life
Stephen Reese

Readers who want to confront their faith more directly, to think it through and be open to God in an individual, authentic, spiritual encounter will find a resonant voice in Stephen Reese.

978-1-57312-553-6 160 pages/pb **$16.00**

Hoping Liberia
Stories of Civil War from Africa's First Republic
John Michael Helms

Through historical narrative, theological ponderings, personal confession, and thoughtful questions, Helms immerses readers into a period of political turmoil and violence, a devastating civil war, and the immeasurable suffering experienced by the Liberian people.

978-1-57312-544-4 208 pages/pb **$18.00**

To order call **1-800-747-3016** or visit **www.helwys.com**

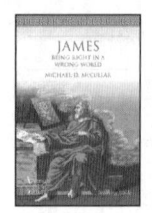

James (Smyth & Helwys Annual Bible Study series)
Being Right in a Wrong World
Michael D. McCullar

Unlike Paul, who wrote primarily to congregations defined by Gentile believers, James wrote to a dispersed and persecuted fellowship of Hebrew Christians who would soon endure even more difficulty in the coming years.

Teaching Guide 1-57312-604-5 160 pages/ pb **$14.00**
Study Guide 1-57312-605-2 96 pages/pb **$6.00**

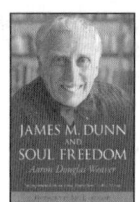

James M. Dunn and Soul Freedom
Aaron Douglas Weaver

James Milton Dunn, over the last fifty years, has been the most aggressive Baptist proponent for religious liberty in the United States. Soul freedom—voluntary uncoerced faith and an unfettered individual conscience before God—is the basis of his understanding of church-state separation and the historic Baptist basis of religious liberty.

978-1-57312-590-1 224 pages/pb **$18.00**

The Jesus Tribe
Following Christ in the Land of the Empire
Ronnie McBrayer

The Jesus Tribe fleshes out the implications, possibilities, contradictions, and complexities of what it means to live within the Jesus Tribe and in the shadow of the American Empire.

978-1-57312-592-5 208 pages/pb **$17.00**

Joint Venture
Jeanie Miley

Joint Venture is a memoir of the author's journey to find and express her inner, authentic self, not as an egotistical venture, but as a sacred responsibility and partnership with God. Miley's quest for Christian wholeness is a rich resource for other seekers.

978-1-57312-581-9 224 pages/pb **$17.00**

Let Me More of Their Beauty See
Reading Familiar Verses in Context
Diane G. Chen

Let Me More of Their Beauty See offers eight examples of how attention to the historical and literary settings can safeguard against taking a text out of context, bring out its transforming power in greater dimension, and help us apply Scripture appropriately in our daily lives.

978-1-57312-564-2 160 pages/pb **$17.00**

To order call **1-800-747-3016** or visit **www.helwys.com**

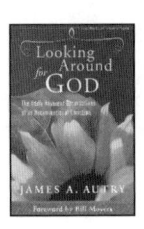

Looking Around for God
The Strangely Reverent Observations of an Unconventional Christian
James A. Autry

Looking Around for God, Autry's tenth book, is in many ways his most personal. In it he considers his unique life of faith and belief in God. Autry is a former Fortune 500 executive, author, poet, and consultant whose work has had a significant influence on leadership thinking.

978-157312-484-3 144 pages/pb **$16.00**

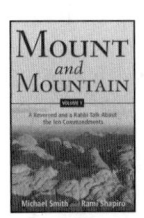

Mount and Mountain
Vol. 1: A Reverend and a Rabbi Talk About the Ten Commandments
Rami Shapiro and Michael Smith

Mount and Mountain represents the first half of an interfaith dialogue—a dialogue that neither preaches nor placates but challenges its participants to work both singly and together in the task of reinterpreting sacred texts. Mike and Rami discuss the nature of divinity, the power of faith, the beauty of myth and story, the necessity of doubt, the achievements, failings, and future of religion, and, above all, the struggle to live ethically and in harmony with the way of God.

978-1-57312-612-0 144 pages/pb **$15.00**

Overcoming Adolescence
Growing Beyond Childhood into Maturity
Marion D. Aldridge

In *Overcoming Adolescence*, Marion Aldridge poses questions for adults of all ages to consider. His challenge to readers is one he has personally worked to confront: to grow up *all the way*—mentally, physically, academically, socially, emotionally, and spiritually. The key not only involves knowing how to work through the process, but how to recognize what may be contributing to our perpetual adolescence.

978-1-57312-577-2 156 pages/pb **$17.00**

Psychic Pancakes & Communion Pizza
More Musings and Mutterings of a Church Misfit
Bert Montgomery

Psychic Pancakes & Communion Pizza is Bert Montgomery's highly anticipated follow-up to *Elvis, Willie, Jesus & Me* and contains further reflections on music, film, culture, life, and finding Jesus in the midst of it all.

978-1-57312-578-9 160 pages/pb **$16.00**

To order call 1-800-747-3016 or visit www.helwys.com

Reading Job (Reading the Old Testament series)
A Literary and Theological Commentary
James L. Crenshaw

At issue in the Book of Job is a question with which most all of us struggle at some point in life, "Why do bad things happen to good people?" James Crenshaw has devoted his life to studying the disturbing matter of theodicy—divine justice—that troubles many people of faith.

978-1-57312-574-1 192 pages/pb **$22.00**

Reading Samuel (Reading the Old Testament series)
A Literary and Theological Commentary
Johanna W. H. van Wijk-Bos

Interpreted masterfully by preeminent Old Testament scholar Johanna W. H. van Wijk-Bos, the story of Samuel touches on a vast array of subjects that make up the rich fabric of human life. The reader gains an inside look at leadership, royal intrigue, military campaigns, occult practices, and the significance of religious objects of veneration.

978-1-57312-607-6 272 pages/pb **$22.00**

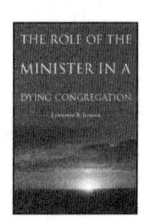

The Role of the Minister in a Dying Congregation
Lynwood B. Jenkins

In *The Role of the Minister in a Dying Congregation* Jenkins provides a courageous and responsible resource on one of the most critical issues in congregational life: how to help a congregation conclude its ministry life cycle with dignity and meaning.

978-1-57312-571-0 96 pages/pb **$14.00**

Sessions with Philippians (Session Bible Studies series)
Finding Joy in Community
Bo Prosser

In this brief letter to the Philippians, Paul makes clear the centrality of his faith in Jesus Christ, his love for the Philippian church, and his joy in serving both Christ and their church.

978-1-57312-579-6 112 pages/pb **$13.00**

To order call **1-800-747-3016** or visit **www.helwys.com**

Sessions with Samuel (Session Bible Studies series)
Stories from the Edge
Tony W. Cartledge

In these stories, Israel faces one crisis after another, a people constantly on the edge. Individuals like Saul and David find themselves on the edge as well, facing troubles of leadership and personal struggle. Yet, each crisis becomes a gateway for learning that God is always present, that hope remains.

978-1-57312-555-0 112 pages/pb **$13.00**

Silver Linings
My Life Before and After Challenger 7
June Scobee Rodgers

We know the public story of *Challenger 7*'s tragic destruction. That day, June's life took a new direction that ultimately led to the creation of the Challenger Center and to new life and new love. Her story of Christian faith and triumph over adversity will inspire readers of every age.

978-1-57312-570-3 352 pages/hc **$28.00**

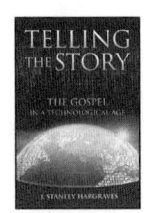

Telling the Story
The Gospel in a Technological Age
J. Stanley Hargraves

From the advent of the printing press to modern church buildings with LCD projectors and computers, the church has adapted the means of communicating the gospel. Adapting that message to the available technology helps the church reach out in meaningful ways to people around the world.

978-1-57312-550-5 112 pages/pb **$14.00**

This is What a Preacher Looks Like
Sermons by Baptist Women in Ministry
Pamela Durso, ed.

A collection of sermons by thirty-six Baptist women, their voices are soft and loud, prophetic and pastoral, humorous and sincere. They are African American, Asian, Latina, and Caucasian. They are sisters, wives, mothers, grandmothers, aunts, and friends.

978-1-57312-554-3 144 pages/pb **$18.00**

To order call **1-800-747-3016** or visit **www.helwys.com**

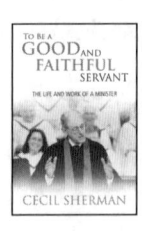

To Be a Good and Faithful Servant
The Life and Work of a Minister

Cecil Sherman

This book offers a window into how one pastor navigated the many daily challenges and opportunities of ministerial life and shares that wisdom with church leaders wherever they are in life—whether serving as lay leaders or as ministers just out of seminary, midway through a career, or seeking renewal after many years of service. 978-1-57312-559-8 208 pages/pb **$20.00**

Transformational Leadership
Leading with Integrity

Charles B. Bugg

"Transformational" leadership involves understanding and growing so that we can help create positive change in the world. This book encourages leaders to be willing to change if *they* want to help transform the world. They are honest about their personal strengths and weaknesses, and are not afraid of doing a fearless moral inventory of themselves.

978-1-57312-558-1 112 pages/pb **$14.00**

Written on My Heart
Daily Devotions for Your Journey through the Bible

Ann H. Smith

Smith takes readers on a fresh and exciting journey of daily readings of the Bible that will change, surprise, and renew you.

978-1-57312-549-9 288 pages/pb **$18.00**

When Crisis Comes Home
Revised and Expanded

John Lepper

The Bible is full of examples of how God's people, with homes grounded in the faith, faced crisis after crisis. These biblical personalities and families were not hopeless in the face of catastrophe—instead, their faith in God buoyed them, giving them hope for the future and strength to cope in the present. John Lepper will help you and your family prepare for, deal with, and learn from crises in your home. 978-1-57312-539-0 152 pages/pb **$17.00**

To order call 1-800-747-3016 or visit www.helwys.com

Cecil Sherman Formations Commentary

Add the wit and wisdom of Cecil Sherman to your library. After 15 years of writing the Smyth & Helwys Formations Commentary, you can now purchase the 5-volume compilation covering the best of Cecil Sherman from Genesis to Revelation.

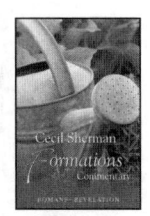

Vol. 1: Genesis–Job   1-57312-476-1 208 pages/pb **$17.00**
Vol. 2: Psalms–Malachi   1-57312-477-X 208 pages/pb **$17.00**
Vol. 3: Matthew–Mark   1-57312-478-8 208 pages/pb **$17.00**
Vol. 4: Luke–Acts   1-57312-479-6 208 pages/pb **$17.00**
Vol. 5: Romans–Revelation   1-57312-480-X 208 pages/pb **$17.00**

To order call **1-800-747-3016** or visit **www.helwys.com**

Clarence Jordan's
Cotton Patch Gospel

The Complete Collection

Hardback • 448 pages

Retail ~~50.00~~ • Your Price 45.00

The Cotton Patch Gospel, by Koinonia Farm founder Clarence Jordan, recasts the stories of Jesus and the letters of the New Testament into the language and culture of the mid-twentieth-century South. Born out of the civil rights struggle, these now-classic translations of much of the New Testament bring the far-away places of Scripture closer to home: Gainesville, Selma, Birmingham, Atlanta, Washington D.C.

More than a translation, *The Cotton Patch Gospel* continues to make clear the startling relevance of Scripture for today. Now for the first time collected in a single, hardcover volume, this edition comes complete with a new Introduction by President Jimmy Carter, a Foreword by Will D. Campbell, and an Afterword by Tony Campolo. Smyth & Helwys Publishing is proud to help reintroduce these seminal works of Clarence Jordan to a new generation of believers, in an edition that can be passed down to generations still to come.

SMYTH & HELWYS

To order call **1-800-747-3016**
or visit **www.helwys.com**